AIA
Architectural Guide to Nassau and Suffolk Counties, Long Island

—— by ——

THE AMERICAN INSTITUTE
OF ARCHITECTS,
LONG ISLAND CHAPTER

—— and ——

THE SOCIETY FOR THE
PRESERVATION OF
LONG ISLAND ANTIQUITIES

DOVER PUBLICATIONS, INC.
New York

EDITORS

Robert B. MacKay
Stanley Lindvall
Carol Traynor

Note: The area code for Nassau and Suffolk Counties is 516.

Published in Canada by General Publishing Company, Ltd., 30 Lesmill Road, Don Mills, Toronto, Ontario.

Published in the United Kingdom by Constable and Company, Ltd., 3 The Lanchesters, 162–164 Fulham Palace Road, London W6 9ER.

AIA Architectural Guide to Nassau and Suffolk Counties, Long Island is a new work, first published by Dover Publications, Inc., in 1992.

Designed by Carol Belanger Grafton

Manufactured in the United States of America
Dover Publications, Inc., 31 East 2nd Street, Mineola, N.Y. 11501

Library of Congress Cataloging-in-Publication Data

AIA architectural guide to Nassau and Suffolk counties, Long Island / by the American Institute of Architects, Long Island Chapter and the Society for the Preservation of Long Island Antiquities.
    p.   cm.
Includes index.
ISBN 0-486-26946-9 (pbk.)
    1. Architecture — New York (State) — Nassau County — Guidebooks. 2. Architecture — New York (State) — Suffolk County — Guidebooks. I. American Institute of Architects, Long Island Chapter. II. Society for the Preservation of Long Island Antiquities.
NA730.N42N372   1992
720'.9747'245 — dc20   91-46261
                                      CIP

Acknowledgments

The monumental task of researching, writing, photographing and assembling this guide could not have been made possible without the concentrated efforts of a team of devoted individuals.

Credit must go first to the Long Island Chapter of the American Institute of Architects for conceiving of this project and for their tireless and enthusiastic commitment, and to its past president, Stanley Lindvall, who began this undertaking and participated in every stage from content to design. Members of the Guidebook Committee included Robert O. MaGraw, John R. Sorrenti, Andrea Briller, William J. Pecau, Peter D'Andrilli and Thomas Hauck, who engineered the cooperation between the committee and SPLIA. Assistance was also provided by AIA members Anthony Musso, Leonard Scheer, Ze'ev Silberman, Thom Penn, James Groark, Monte Leeper, Joseph Hopke, Ron Goodman, Neal Hoffman, Harry Eng, Hans Nepf, Robert Bayley and Richard Suter. Carol Traynor, the Society's publications coordinator, filled many roles in the preparation of this text, from writing and research to organization.

Special thanks are due to our 16 contributing authors who brought diverse and unique skills to bear on this project: Zachary Studenroth, a student of Long Island's early architecture, also helped in selecting the entries for the guide with Barbara Van Liew; Alastair Gordon shared his knowledge of, and research on, Modernist Long Island buildings; appreciation is also extended to contributors Dr. Roger G. Gerry, Carl Starace, Robert Hefner, Elizabeth L. Watson, Carolyn Oldenbusch, Ellen Williams, Susan Davenport, Hugh Jay Gershon, Kurt Kahofer, Edward J. Smits, Kitt Barrett, Jay Graybeal, Nick Langhart and Ellen Fletcher.

Joseph Adams and Mary Ann Spencer contributed their talents as photographers. Many individuals and institutions were generous in supplying reference materials and photographs to assist us, particularly the Roslyn Landmark Society, Richard Winsche of the Nassau County Museum Reference Library and the Long Island State Park Region. Nor would this undertaking have been possible without the encouragement and sage counsel of SPLIA's Publication Committee and Hayward Cirker, Dover's publisher and a lifelong architecture buff.

THE EDITORS

CONTRIBUTORS

Unless otherwise specified, references are to article numbers.

AG (Alastair Gordon), 29, 35, 37, 51, 94, 98, 104, 105, 106, 113, 126, 131, 134, 135, 152, 154, 167, 182, 183, 193, 249, p. 102

CO (Carolyn Oldenbusch), 147, 148, 149, 150

CS (Carl Starace), 107

CT (Carol Traynor), 1, 5, 7, 24, 26, 27, 32, 33, 40, 45, 46, 53, 55, 60, 65, 66, 78, 87, 88, 112, 114, 115, 144, 158, 159, 160, 161, 163, 165, 166, 180, 185, 216, 224, 231, 235, 236, 239, 243, 244, 245

EF (Ellen Fletcher), 3, 12, 13, 17, 28, 30, 47, 48, 49, 50, 56, 58, 69, 90, 117, 124, 125, 127, 132, 155, 162, 186, 197, 198, 200, 201, 202, 203, 204, 205, 206, 207, 208, 209, 210, 211, 214, 226, 228, 229, 232, 233, 238, 246

EJS (Edward J. Smits), p. 48

ELW (Elizabeth L. Watson), 170, pp. 90/91

EW (Ellen Williams), 99, 100, 108, 116

HJG (Hugh Jay Gershon), 19

JAG (Jay A. Graybeal), 121, 122, 133

KB (Kitt Barrett), 59, 64, 103, 119, 120, 136, 173, 174, 189, 199, 213, 218, 219, 227, 234

KK (Kurt Kahofer), 250

NL (Nicholas Langhart), 212, 215, 220, 221, 222, 223, 241

RBM (Robert B. MacKay), 2, 4, 8, 9, 10, 11, 14, 15, 16, 18, 20, 21, 22, 23, 25, 34, 36, 38, 39, 43, 44, 54, 57, 61, 62, 63, 67, 80, 89, 91, 92, 96, 97, 101, 109, 123, 130, 140, 145, 151, 171, 176, 177, 178, 190, 191, 192, 195, 196, 225, 230, 242, 248, p. 10, p. 20, pp. 32/33, pp. 70/71, p. 134

RGG (Dr. Roger G. Gerry), 70, 71, 72, 73, 74, 75, 76, 77, 79, 81, 82, 83, 84, 85, 86

RH (Robert Hefner), 102, 128, 141, 181, 184, p. 78

SJD (Susan J. Davenport), 175

ZS (Zachary Studenroth), 6, 31, 41, 42, 52, 68, 93, 95, 110, 111, 118, 129, 137, 138, 139, 142, 143, 146, 153, 156, 157, 164, 168, 169, 172, 179, 187, 188, 194, 217, 237, 240, 247, 251, 252, pp. 160/161

PHOTOGRAPHIC SOURCES AND CREDITS

Unless otherwise specified, references are to article
numbers and associated illustrations.

INTRODUCTION

While Newport may have more opulent mansions, Southern California more examples of the Modern Movement and Boston's North Shore a greater concentration of early or First Period buildings, few parts of the country can boast the range and depth of domestic architecture that can be found on Long Island. Perhaps because the Industrial Revolution bypassed the region for lack of falling water to power mill turbines, Long Island's built environment was not seriously affected by subsequent development from the seventeenth century until the post–World War II period, when the G. I. Bill and the growth of the aircraft industry sent thousands eastward on Robert Moses' parkways toward new suburban communities such as Levittown. As a result, Long Island possesses close to 100 First Period buildings (a number second only to Essex County, Massachusetts), the greatest concentration of surviving windmills and tide mills (the alternatives to falling water), most of its eighteenth-century manorial seats and dozens of relatively intact nineteenth-century villages. Of the architect-designed country houses built here between the Civil War and World War II, 550 survive, filling a wide spectrum of adaptive reuses. As a birthplace of suburbia, the region's innovations range from highway improvements to novel shopping centers and airports. Long Island is also significant for its Modern and Post-Modern architecture, the South Fork in particular having served as an incubator for progressive domestic design for over a century.

By another yardstick — the number of commissions by the leading architects of their eras — Long Island also boasts impressive statistics. Before the Civil War, architect-designed buildings east of the present-day city line were rare, notably Minard Lafever's work in Sag Harbor and Town & Davis' Rockaway Pavilion. However, the discovery of the region's resort potential in the 1860s and 1870s led to the appearance of country seats by such talented practitioners as the Central Park collaborators Calvert Vaux and Jacob Wrey Mould, along with Detlef Lenau, Bruce Price, James Renwick and Richard Morris Hunt. By the 1880s, McKim, Mead & White were at work on what would eventually comprise some two-score commissions within the region, including such seminal designs as Clarence Mackey's palatial "Harbour Court" and the Garden City Hotel (both demolished). The decades spanning the turn of the century, which coincided with the region's ascendency as the national resort, brought the greatest talent in the land to Long Island and witnessed a remarkable number of country-house commissions by such prominent firms as Carrère & Hastings (18), Delano and Aldrich (23) and John Russell Pope (20). One of Modernism's showcases, the 1939 World's Fair at Flushing Meadows, has left us with such treasures as Kocher & Frey's Aluminaire House. Other designs of the 1930s and 1940s are Frank Lloyd Wright's Rebhuhn House, Marcel Breuer's Geller House and Wallace K. Harrison's own house. From the 1950s we have commissions by Philip Johnson, Richard Neutra, Peter Blake, Edward Durell Stone and José Luis Sert, while in the 1960s and 1970s Long Island's domestic legacy was enriched by the work of Gwathmey & Siegel, Robert A. M. Stern, Julian and Barbara Neski, Richard Meier and Norman Jaffe.

The hardest task of the editors has been to select 252 buildings from Nassau and Suffolk counties (Queens and Brooklyn being covered in the *AIA Guide to New York City*), where over 7000 structures still stand that were built before the twentieth century. Unquestionably, there are buildings that have been omitted that deserve to be included here and, hence, we see this project as being incomplete and look forward to a second edition to this guide in which more structures will be represented. The Society for the Preservation of Long Island Antiquities (SPLIA), 93 North Country Road, Setauket, NY 11733, will maintain files for future nominations and welcomes the reader's participation in the nomination process.

ROBERT B. MACKAY

LONG ISLAND

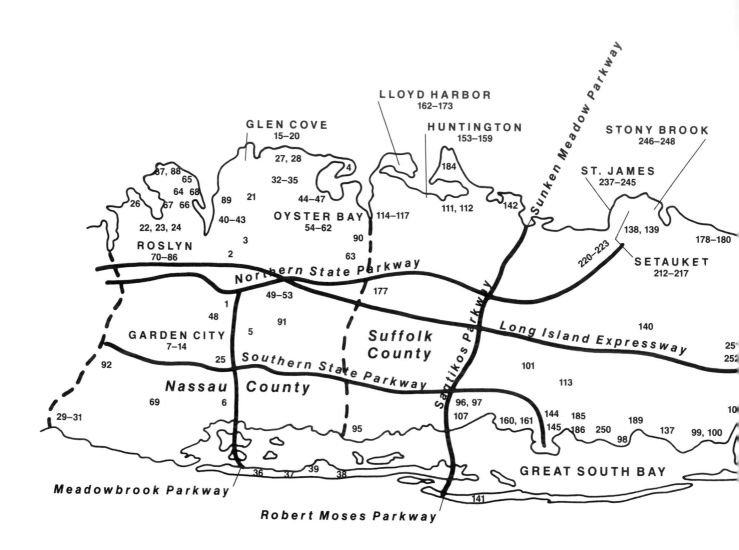

LLOYD HARBOR
162–173

GLEN COVE
15–20

HUNTINGTON
153–159

STONY BROOK
246–248

27, 28

4

ST. JAMES
237–245

87, 88
65
64 68
67 66

89
21

32–35

184

44–47

138, 139

26

138, 139

22, 23, 24

40–43

OYSTER BAY
54–62

114–117

111, 112

142

178–180

ROSLYN
70–86

3

90

220–223

SETAUKET
212–217

2

63

Northern State Parkway

177

Sunken Meadow Parkway

1

49–53

Long Island Expressway

140

48

91

25'

GARDEN CITY
7–14

5

Suffolk
County

252

25

Southern State Parkway

Santikos Parkway

101

92

Nassau   County

113

69

6

96, 97

144

185

189

107

160, 161

145

186

250

98

137

99, 100

29–31

95

10

GREAT SOUTH BAY

36

37

39

38

Meadowbrook Parkway

141

Robert Moses Parkway

The numbers on the map refer to articles in the text.
For page numbers see the contents, pp. xiii–xvii.

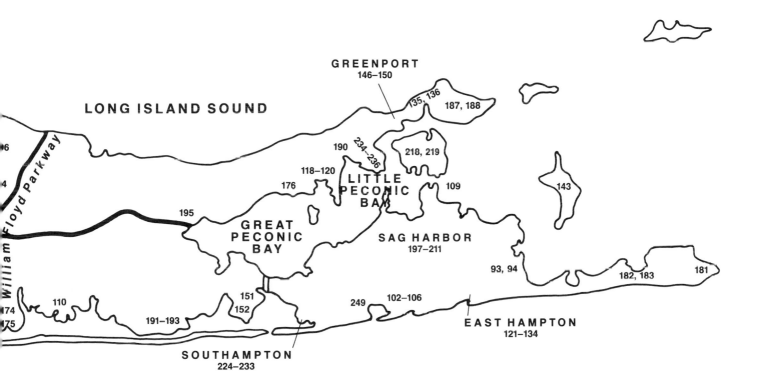

GREENPORT
146–150

LONG ISLAND SOUND

135, 136   187, 188

William Floyd Parkway

190   234–236   218, 219

118–120

176   LITTLE PECONIC BAY   109

195

GREAT PECONIC BAY

SAG HARBOR
197–211

143

93, 94   182, 183   181

110   151   249   102–106

152   EAST HAMPTON
121–134

191–193

SOUTHAMPTON
224–233

ATLANTIC OCEAN

CONTENTS

SUFFOLK COUNTY

ESSAYS

Contents

NASSAU

1. RELIANCE FEDERAL SAVINGS AND LOAN ASSOCIATION

Willis Avenue and I.U. Willets Road, Albertson. An almost pie-shaped piece of property at the intersection of Willis Avenue and I.U. Willets Road dictated the circular plan for a dramatic and innovative small-branch building of the Reliance Federal Savings and Loan Association. Lightweight steel framing and a stucco curtain wall were utilized by architect Siegmund Spiegel for this 80-foot-diameter building, which opened in 1967. The first floor, housing the main banking complex, is 68 feet in diameter. The upper floor, housing offices around the periphery, is cantilevered six feet beyond the first floor. Dramatic elements employed by the architect include a rotunda 300 feet in diameter topped by a sky dome that allows light to reach the main banking floor. A brick curved pylon wall at the entrance conveniently houses a vault, stairs, boardroom and the mechanical components of the building. (CT)

2. HILLWOOD COMMONS STUDENT UNION FACILITY

Long Island University, C.W. Post Campus, Northern Boulevard, Brookville (open to the public). The Hillwood Commons Student Union Facility was the 1974 recipient of the Long Island Chapter of the AIA's Gold Archi Award. Designed by the Locust Valley firm of Bentel and Bentel, the huge facility, comprised of offices, meeting rooms, lounges, food service facilities, a 300-seat cinema, 500-seat lecture hall and bookshop, was sympathetically introduced into its setting in such a way as not to impinge upon the great lawn of the campus or compete with the existing buildings. Kiosks at the entrances are the only indication of the structure, which is situated behind a forested ridge linking parking areas to the campus in a restrained and imaginative fashion. (RBM)

3

3. SAMUEL A. SALVAGE HOUSE (NOW VILLA BANFI IMPORTERS)

Cedar Swamp Road, Brookville (not open to the public). The London-born Sir Samuel Agar Salvage, pioneer promoter of rayon, commissioned Roger H. Bullard to design this rambling, asymmetrical limestone mansion. Later owners, before the estate became the corporate headquarters for a major wine importer, included Mrs. Alfred G. Vanderbilt (wife of the Commodore's great-great-grandson) and Frederick W. Lundy, Sheepshead Bay restaurateur. Completed in 1927, the Elizabethan style "Rynwood" has a U-shaped main block with a grass court nestled between the arms on its south side. The disposition of bays, gables and entrance porch logically expresses the interior arrangement. Formal gardens adjoin the house to the west, with a service court to the east. The estate complex includes the mansion with its service wings, an award-winning gatehouse, bridges and walls along the driveway, garage, greenhouse and two garden buildings. The "Rynwood" garden, designed by landscape architect Ellen Shipman, was known as one of the finest on Long Island. (EF)

4. SEAWANHAKA CORINTHIAN YACHT CLUB

Yacht Club Road, Centre Island (private club — not open to the public). Architects rarely get to choose the sites for buildings they are commissioned to design, but Robert W. Gibson (1854–1927) had that opportunity with the Seawanhaka Corinthian Yacht Club's Centre Island station. Gibson, an accomplished canoe sailor, was cruising the North Shore looking for a location for a canoe-club camp in mid-summer of 1889 when he first discovered the site. Two years later construction had commenced on the substantial Shingle Style clubhouse for the Manhattan-based yacht club, which Gibson had recently joined. Colonial Revival symmetry and detailing characterize the composition of this fine example of clubhouse architecture of the period. It is shown here on opening day, May 28, 1892. Gibson, an Englishman, had trained at the Royal Academy of Arts where he was awarded the Soane Medallion. Among his better-known commissions were Morton F. Plant's Fifth Avenue town house (now the Cartier building) and Albany's Episcopal Cathedral, won in a famous competition in which the plans of the leading architect of the time, H. H. Richardson, were rejected. (RBM)

5. NASSAU COUNTY MEDICAL CENTER

2201 Hempstead Turnpike, East Meadow. The Nassau County Medical Center has served the health needs of the community for over 50 years. In the early 1960s, an ambitious program was begun to upgrade the entire complex in a three-stage construction program. The result was a ten-year Master Plan under the supervision of Max Urbahn and Urbahn Associates for the demolition, expansion and modernization of existing buildings coupled with the construction of urgently needed new facilities. Today the imposing brick Medical Center includes a new staff-housing and activities complex and maintenance facilities, a 715-bed teaching hospital and space for psychiatric care, home care and hospital-community-based welfare programs spatially arranged in three soaring wings. With over 45 years of practice, Urbahn Associates has worked on projects all over the world and in such diversified categories as residential, transportation, medical, research-and-development and educational. (CT)

4

5

Centre Island / East Meadow

5

6

6. BROOKLYN WATERWORKS

Sunrise Highway (north side), Freeport (can be seen from the road). Monumental in scale and lavish in its ornamentation of cut and molded brick detail, the Brooklyn Waterworks in Freeport is unquestionably Long Island's most ambitious Romanesque Revival design. Formerly known as the Milburn Pumping Station, the three-story brick structure is the work of Frank Freeman (1852–1940), the noted Brooklyn architect whose Eagle Warehouse and Storage Company (1893) and City of Brooklyn Fire Headquarters (1892) are noted as two of the city's most powerful Richardsonian commissions. The waterworks was conceived as a part of the extensive system that brought Nassau County water into Brooklyn in the late nineteenth and early twentieth centuries. Abandoned in the 1920s, the conduit line was soon after utilized as a right-of-way for the Sunrise Highway, which opened in 1928. The waterworks was decommissioned and kept in reserve for emergency use by the City of New York until its sale to Nassau County in 1977. Today the structure, privately owned, awaits sympathetic rehabilitation. (ZS)

7. NASSAU COMMUNITY COLLEGE

Stewart Avenue, Garden City (accessible to the public). Completed in 1978 and designed by David L. Finci of The Eggers Group PC, the sprawling "megastructure" of Nassau Community College houses the Administration and Maintenance Buildings, the Library, the Physical Education and Sport Center and two academic wings. Dominated by the 12-story Administration Tower, the entire complex is based on 20-foot-wide structural bays of precast, prestressed concrete components with spans ranging from 20 to 125 feet, permitting easy expansion of the original core. The site plan for the 226 acres, formerly the site of Mitchel Field, retains much of the area as open space for parking and outdoor recreation. Since its inception in 1960 with 632 students who attended classes in a wing of the Mineola Court House, Nassau Community College has become one of the nation's largest two-year colleges, with over 20,000 students. (CT) *7: Library (left) with Administration Tower in background. 7A: Academic wing.*

7

7A

8

9

8. NORSTAR BANK

1035 Stewart Avenue, Garden City. Originally designed as both the executive headquarters and a branch office of the Hempstead Bank, Norstar Bank at 1035 Stewart Avenue in Garden City received the Long Island Chapter of the AIA's Silver Archi Award in 1972. By canting the street facade, architects Maria and Frederick Bentel sought to lessen the constraints on the subse-quent development of the adjoining parcels of land while providing private terraces for the executive offices. The salient interior feature is a dramatic three-story brick-walled courtyard replete with Mexican tile floors and abundant plantings to give, in the architects' words, "employees and patrons the possibility of experiencing and sharing the totality of the building." (RBM)

9. THE SWIRBUL LIBRARY

Adelphi University, South Avenue, Garden City (accessible to the public). One of the great figures of the Modern movement in America, the California architect Richard J. Neutra (1892–1970), co-designed Adelphi University's Leon A. Swirbul Library, opened to the public August 16, 1963. The exterior of the 36,881-square-foot two-story brick, aluminum and reinforced-concrete modular learning center is typical of the rather stark and mechanistic work of Neutra and his partner, the planner Robert Alex-ander, in this period. Inside, however, their artistry is immediately apparent in features such as the dramatic freestanding staircase, which Neutra designed to symbolize "the spiraled ascent to wisdom." Neutra, the first architect to appear on the cover of *Time*, specialized in learning centers and wrote that the "vibrant life" concealed in libraries "must be the conviction of the architect." (RBM)

10. RUTH S. HARLEY UNIVERSITY CENTER

Adelphi University, South Avenue, Garden City (accessible to the public). The dynamically massed Ruth S. Harley University Center at Adelphi University received a Certificate of Merit from the New York State Association of Architects in 1971, the year it was completed, and an Archi Award the same year. Designed by Warner Burns Toan & Lunde, a Manhattan firm that specializes in library and collegiate projects, the 70,000-square-foot building is formed around a three-story atrium and houses dozens of university functions, ranging from the campus radio station and rathskeller to a 700-seat auditorium. Among this firm's other Long Island commissions are Hofstra University's 1967 pedestrian bridge and library. (RBM)

---

11. ENDO LABORATORIES, INC.

1000 Stewart Avenue, Garden City (private company — can be seen from the road). One of Long Island's most acclaimed post-World War II buildings is Endo Laboratories' 1969 Garden City facility. It's architect, Paul Rudolph, a former dean of Yale's department of architecture, sought to break out of the usual factory format. In place of the formula of boxlike office in front and plant behind, Rudolph created a facility in which the manufacturing functions are located in the lower and middle levels; offices and a cafeteria above open onto a roof garden. Staircases and HVAC ducts are located at the edges of the structure inside the turrets, which resemble those of a medieval fortress, allowing for uninterrupted floor space and interior amenities such as a dramatic multilevel lobby. On the exterior, the silhouette is irregular, sculptural and even "sinuous," thought *Life* in 1971, thanks to the terraced levels of curving concrete, all of which display the corduroylike textural surfaces that are a Rudolph hallmark. As in most of Rudolph's work, Endo Laboratories stimulates and delights but never overwhelms or confines. (RBM)

10

11

GARDEN CITY

A

B

C

*G*arden City was planned as a model village providing "pleasant and reasonable" housing on a rental basis for the employees of its creator, Manhattan dry-goods merchant and hotel owner Alexander Turney Stewart (1801–1876). Stewart's purchase of 7000 acres of the Hempstead Plains in 1869 launched a development project that was unprecedented in the Long Island experience. Architect John Kellum, a native of Hempstead who had designed Stewart's Manhattan store and Fifth Avenue residence, oversaw the design and construction of a community that was soon comprised of houses, stores and carriage drives surrounding a 30-acre park with a hotel. There was even a branch railroad line and station. Later came great memorial projects: the Cathedral of the Incarnation (1883, *see* No. 12), the Bishop's palace (1880) and St. Paul's (1879, *see* No. 14) and St. Mary's (1892) schools.

However, following Stewart's death in 1876 (and Kellum's in 1871), Garden City was to languish until McKim, Mead & White's reconstruction of the hotel (1900–01), the laying out of W. K. Vanderbilt's Long Island Motor Parkway, the growth of aviation on the Hempstead Plains and the general development of the Island as a resort and suburb focused renewed attention on the village. Beginning in 1907, Garden City Estates was developed on land west of St. Paul's School on a plan by noted landscape architects Charles W. Leavitt, Jr., and Cyril E. Marshall. Three years later, Doubleday, Page and Company [*see* No. 13] chose the village as the site for the Country Life Press, their impressive publishing plant in the image of England's Hampton Court, designed by the architectural firm of Kirby & Petit. Doubleday was also behind the development of Franklin Court, the model housing development (ca. 1912) bordering the train tracks south of the village. (RBM)

A: View of Garden City, ca. 1875. B: One of the "Twelve Apostle" houses. C: Garden City Hotel, ca. 1920. D: Garden City Hotel, designed by Theodore Bindrim, 1978.

D

12A

12. THE CATHEDRAL OF THE INCARNATION

50 Cathedral Avenue (corner of sixth Avenue), Garden City (open to the public). When Garden City was planned, no provision was made for a church. But shortly after its founder Alexander Turney Stewart died in 1876, his widow, Cornelia Clinch Stewart, decided to establish one in his memory. Although Mrs. Stewart had a detailed vision for the building itself — an ornate white marble structure in the Gothic Revival style set amid a green and flowering landscape — she did not specify its denomination. In 1877, Mrs. Stewart radically elevated the original concept of a memorial church when she proposed that it replace Holy Trinity in Brooklyn as the cathedral for the Protestant Episcopal diocese of Long Island, thus requiring a more elaborate structure. As architect, she chose English-born Henry G. Harrison (1813–1895), who was influenced by A. N. W. Pugin and was a favorite architect of the Episcopal Church. For eight years, from 1876 through 1883, the great church of Garden City rose (210 feet to the spire's tip), was ornamented and finally completed in the Perpendicular Gothic style of the fourteenth century. The cathedral now anchors an ecclesiastical complex including a see house, a chapter house and the other appointments of a complete cathedral organization on the English model. (EF) *12A: A view of 1915.*

13

14

13. DOUBLEDAY, PAGE AND COMPANY (ALSO CALLED COUNTRY LIFE PRESS)

Franklin Avenue, between Second & Sixth Streets, Garden City. In 1910, just after the Queensboro Bridge (connecting with Northern Boulevard) made the North Shore of Long Island more accessible than ever before, the publishing house of Doubleday, Page and Company moved to the planned town of Garden City. Kirby & Petit designed a two-and-a-half-story brick-and-stone plant on Franklin Avenue, Tudor Revival in style and collegiate in appearance, housing offices and printing plant under a single roof. Surrounded by gardens landscaped by Leonard Barron, Country Life Press was a welcome addition to the town. Soon the plant had its own stop on the Long Island Rail Road, and a cluster of inexpensive employee houses (designed by Garden City Hotel builders Ford, Butler & Oliver) on nearby Franklin Court. During World War II, the plant was enlarged and its gardens turned into parking lots, and in 1956 the entire structure was converted to publishing office space. (EF)

14. ST. PAUL'S SCHOOL

295 Stewart Avenue, Garden City (private school — can be seen from the road). Built as a memorial to department-store magnate Alexander Turney Stewart in 1879, St. Paul's School was from the outset an extraordinary structure. Designed by Edward H. Harris in the Ruskinian Gothic Style, a mode rarely encountered outside of an urban context, the huge mansard-roofed brick building, with its ornate 300-foot facade, 500 rooms and fenestration comprised of 642 windows, was, on its completion, Long Island's largest structure other than a resort hotel. Polychromatic voussoir-arched windows, elaborate cast-iron balustrades and Dorchester stone trim were some of the elements that combined to make St. Paul's such a successful exercise in Victorian exuberance. It is shown here in a view of ca. 1910. A military academy until 1895, St. Paul's boasted all necessary facilities under one roof, including a chapel patterned after that of an English public school, classrooms, laboratories, a gymnasium, armory and subbasement large enough to function as a drill or parade ground during inclement weather. Today the landmark building continues to serve the needs of one of Long Island's finest preparatory schools. (RBM)

15. PRATT MAUSOLEUM

Old Tappen Road, Glen Cove (private — not open to the public). Old family burial grounds are frequently encountered on Long Island, but Dosoris Cemetery, the beautifully landscaped estate-period private graveyard of the Pratt family in Lattingtown, is unique. At its center is the monumentally scaled Romanesque Revival mausoleum (1892–96) of Charles Pratt, the founder of the family fortune, who was John D. Rockefeller's partner at Standard Oil. Designed by William B. Tubby (1858–1944), the pink granite structure is comprised of a tower and crypt joined by a "bridge of sighs." The Tiffany Glass and Decorating Company was responsible for the richly ornamented interior and its striking mosaics. Seven of Charles Pratt's eight children, whose Dosoris Park estates stood to the west of the mausoleum, are interred in the cemetery, as are many of their children. (RBM) *15: Exterior. 15A: Interior.*

16. "KILLENWORTH," GEORGE D. PRATT HOUSE

Dosoris Lane, Glen Cove (not open to the public). Judged "the best house of the year" in 1914 by the popular periodical *Country Life in America*, "Killenworth" has again been the focus of national publicity in recent years as the country retreat of the Soviet Union's United Nations delegation. It was designed for conservationist George D. Pratt by the architectural firm of Trowbridge & Ackerman. Both partners in the firm spent a month living in the previous house on the site in order to study local conditions including the "breezes, views, grades and approach, etc." "Killenworth" is a majestic Tudor Revival mansion built of blue-gray seam-faced Massachusetts granite with Indiana limestone trim. Sited on a rise to take advantage of the prevailing southeast breeze and with views of Long Island Sound to the north, the carefully landscaped and terraced grounds include a tree-lined forecourt, sunken service court and immense pool. "Killenworth" was one of 13 mansions in the Dosoris area of Glen Cove built by descendants of Charles Pratt. (RBM)

17. "WINFIELD HALL," FRANK W. WOOLWORTH HOUSE

Crescent Beach Road, Glen Cove (Pall Corporation — not open to the public). Five-and-dime magnate F. W. Woolworth commissioned C. P. H. Gilbert to design this spectacular marble mansion after an earlier house on the site (also designed by Gilbert) burned down in 1916. Gilbert, Beaux-Arts trained and experienced in tycoons' town and country houses, had previously designed Woolworth's Fifth Avenue residence as well as several houses in Glen Cove's "North Country Colony," where Woolworth bought an estate in 1914. Woolworth, who died shortly after his house was completed, involved himself intimately in the design of "Winfield Hall," insisting on a catalogue of architectural styles for the upstairs rooms, ranging from Louis XIV through Adam to Chinoiserie. The house itself is a highly formal Italianate villa, set on a knoll that commands formal gardens and a terraced slope overlooking the Sound, and has recently been readapted to corporate use. (EF) *17: The main facade. 17A: The garden facade.*

17A

17

Glen Cove

15

18

19

Glen Cove

16

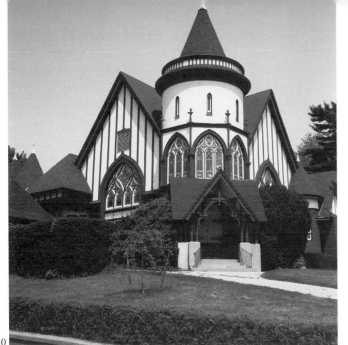

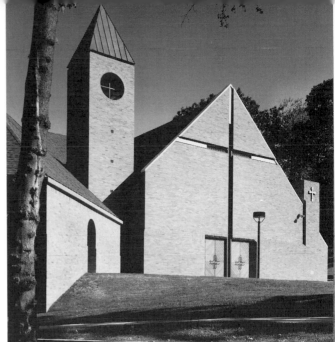

18. "THE BRAES," HERBERT L. PRATT HOUSE (NOW WEBB INSTITUTE)

Crescent Beach Road, Glen Cove (private institution — not open to the public). "The Braes" (Scottish for hillside), built in 1912 by Herbert L. Pratt, Chairman of the Standard Oil Company of New York (SOCONY) and the youngest son of oil magnate Charles Pratt, was the largest mansion in the Pratt family compound at Glen Cove known as Dosoris Park. Replacing an earlier wood-frame Colonial Revival country house, Herbert's second domicile on the site was built in brick and designed by James Brite (d. 1942) on an H-plan in the Jacobean Revival style. Noted landscape architect James L. Greenleaf (1857–1933) was responsible for the carefully terraced grounds descending to Long Island Sound, and Charles of London, the decorator and brother of the famous art dealer Joseph Duveen, may have had a hand in its furnishing. Since 1945 "The Braes" has been the home of the Webb Institute for Naval Architecture. (RBM)

19. "THE MANOR," JOHN PRATT HOUSE (NOW HARRISON CONFERENCE CENTER)

Dosoris Lane, Glen Cove. The 1910 55 acre estate of John and Ruth Pratt was considered by *Country Life* magazine as one of the "best twelve country houses in America." Designed by noted architect Charles Adam Platt, the brick Georgian mansion, set in pastoral surroundings, was an integral part of the many glamorous estates that comprised Long Island's Gold Coast. John Pratt, who died in 1927, was an attorney and executive with Standard Oil Company. His wife, Ruth Baker Pratt, was the first Republican Congresswoman from the State of New York, representing New York City's "Silk Stocking" district. Ruth and her family maintained the estate until her death in 1965. Since the acquisition of the estate by the Harrison Conference Services in 1967, additions and conversions sympathetic to the original structure have succeeded in creating one of the premier conference centers in the country. In 1985 Harrison was recognized as one of the eight best conference centers by readers of *Corporate Meetings and Incentives* magazine. It has also been used as a location for the films *North by Northwest*, *Sabrina Fair* and *Where's Poppa?* (HJG)

20. THE FIRST PRESBYTERIAN CHURCH

School Street at North Lane, Glen Cove (open to the public). Glen Cove's First Presbyterian Church was built in 1905 to the designs of Oscar S. Teale, a New York and New Jersey ecclesiastical architect, who had a long and prolific career. After receiving his diploma from Cooper Union in 1866, Teale trained in a number of New York architectural offices including that of J. Cleveland Cady and Lamb & Rich, architects of "Sagamore Hill." On his own from 1882 to 1927, Teale undertook commissions including the Lewis Avenue Congregational Church in Brooklyn, the Centenary Collegiate Institute at Hackettstown, New Jersey, and the Houdini Monument at the Cypress Hills Cemetery in Brooklyn. At Glen Cove, Teale took advantage of a dramatic site on a rise at the north end of School Street, placing the Tudor Revival church on a diagonal axis with a corner entrance. He then employed the strong forms of two gables and a corner tower to compose this picturesque but balanced design. The handsome church is representative of the wealth of architect-designed churches, which were being built on both the North and South Shores at the turn of the century as the resort movement swelled congregations and created an ecclesiastical building boom. (RBM)

21. ST. HYACINTH R.C. CHURCH

319 Cedar Swamp Road, Glen Head. Designed by Bentel and Bentel and winner of a 1988 Archi Award, this church was built in 1986. A substantial effort was made by the designers to include subtle features from Middle European/Polish churches. The brick detailing, the heavy plank front door and oval windows with wrought-iron grillwork are a few of the elements that are used to give St. Hyacinth's its distinctive quality. However, the church derives its character from its masonry construction. In its detailing, the masonry work is intended to enhance the qualities of scale and texture so important to the ambience of this religious space. The tower, which is the focus of the exterior composition, is also experienced internally, its base forming the connection between the chapel and the vestibule. (RBM)

22. GREAT NECK PUBLIC LIBRARY

Bayview Avenue and Grist Mill Lane, Great Neck (open to the public). Solid, functional and attractive, the library at the corner of Bayview Avenue and Grist Mill Lane in Great Neck is a civic achievement on the part of a community that takes its institutions of learning seriously. Designed by Gibbons, Heidtman and Salvador, the 47,100-square-foot library was built in 1968 and received awards for excellence in architecture from both the Long Island Association of Business & Commerce and the New York State Association of Architects. In 1970 it won an Archi Award.

Characterized on the exterior by rubble stone piers and recessed window bays, the learning center is also noteworthy for an unusual interior feature, "Levels," a youth facility and meeting place completed in 1974 to the designs of Michael Harris Spector. Described as a "series of levels, steps, spaces, nooks, platforms, recesses, expanses and possibilities" where youth can meet, talk and be creative, "Levels" also received an award the year it was completed from the Long Island Chapter of the AIA. (RBM)

23. REHBUHN HOUSE

9a Myrtle Drive (East of Bayview), Great Neck (private residence — not open to the public). One of Long Island's architectural surprises is a Frank Lloyd Wright house in Great Neck. Built between 1936 and 1937 for publisher Ben Rehbuhn and his wife, Ann, the sweepingly horizontal wood, brick and glass structure harkens more to the architect's early Prairie School work than the flat-roofed, do-it-yourself "Usonian" houses he was to introduce at about the same time with the first Jacobs House in 1937.

Edgar Tafel, a student at Wright's Taliesin Fellowship during these years, completed the working drawings after Wright had made the initial design. Tafel, who was also to make several site visits during construction, wondered in later years why Wright had not chosen a more experimental design, noting that the great architect may have "feared he couldn't get something more original built in the East [or] felt it was more in the Rehbuhns' style." (RBM)

22

23

24

24. SADDLE ROCK GRIST MILL

Grist Mill Lane, Great Neck (closed for restoration; scheduled to reopen in 1992). The earliest documentation for a mill on this site dates to 1702 when Robert Hubbs, Jr. of Madnan's Neck (the present Great Neck) sold one half of the mill to Henry Allen. Allen, a prosperous farmer and merchant, acquired complete control in 1715, he and his descendants operated the mill until the 1820s, when it passed to Richard Udall, remaining in the hands of the Udall family until the 1950s. Much of the mill was known to have been rebuilt after a fire in 1715 and again in 1790 following neglect occasioned by the Revolution, and it is not clear how much of the early mill survives in the present structure. The machinery in the four-story building includes many cast-iron parts that replaced earlier wooden machinery, including stone nuts and cup elevators, probably installed during the Udall ownership in the nineteenth century when American milling was revolutionized by the work of Owen Evans, inventor of many devices to automate mills. By the late nineteenth century, however, Long Island farmers ceased to produce large amounts of grain, and mills like Saddle Rock fell into disuse. Acquired by Nassau County's Department of Parks and Recreation in the 1950s, the mill was opened as a museum in 1961. Currently closed, the mill will reopen again in 1992 as a working example of the principal industry of rural Long Island in the seventeenth and eighteenth centuries. (CT)

25. ST. GEORGE'S CHURCH

319 Front Street, Hempstead (open to the public). Modeled after its minister's former parish church in Connecticut, the majestic Federal style St. George's Episcopal Church in Hempstead was built between 1822 and 1823 to replace a 1734 house of worship that stood nearby. William Rhodes, the master carpenter, set up a huge lathe at the site to turn the 30-foot columns that support the interior galleries. The clock tower, with its domed octagonal belfry, is reminiscent of Setauket's First Presbyterian Church of 1813, while the semicircular arched windows with interlocking muntins at the gallery level create a Gothic effect and enliven the fenestration. High atop sits a weather vane recycled from the 1734 church, said to be pierced by bullet holes made by British soldiers holding target practice during the Revolution. The ca. 1822 rectory, located at Prospect and Greenwich Streets, is a handsome five-bay dwelling exhibiting a Dutch-Colonial gambrel roof, a Palladian window and other architectural features once frequently encountered on western Long Island. (RBM)

JONES BEACH

A

C

Jones Beach State Park, end of
Meadowbrook Parkway, Wantagh

*E*ven half a century after its completion, Jones Beach remains one of the greatest public construction achievements of the twentieth century. It was conceived on a scale that could only have been comprehended by its creator, Robert Moses. The world's largest public recreational facility, it opened in August 1929, and covered six miles of ocean frontage on which there were 78 acres of parking fields, two great bathing pavilions (the westernmost of which provided lockers for 15,000 visitors), restaurants, a marine theater and myriad other facilities — all connected by a 17-mile Ocean Parkway, and from 1934 on accessed by the world's first fully divided limited-access highway, the Meadowbrook Parkway. In Lincolnesque fashion Moses was to plan the whole complex in just a few minutes on the back of an envelope on which he sketched the two bathhouses linked by the Parkway and boardwalk but separated by a central turning circle in which the water tower was to be located. Moses' staff architect, Herbert A. Magoon, was the principal designer of the seaside facilities, which were built of Briar Hill sandstone and pink Barbizon brick in a Neo-Gothic mode of the Art Deco Style. Construction was to continue for a decade after the completion of the initial building, the West Bathhouse (1929), largely as Works Progress Administration projects. Attention to detail and imagination characterized the design of even the smallest features at Jones Beach, such as the trash cans, which resemble ships' funnels, and the charming signs that conveyed their messages in letters and silhouettes. The Water Tower (1930), a 200-foot copper-roofed obelisk inspired by the campanile of St. Mark's in Venice, has come to symbolize Jones Beach for thousands of Long Islanders who can see its lights at night from distances as great as 25 miles. Architecture critic Paul Goldberger has noted that the tower belongs more in the category of World's Fair theme structures and that its real function is to alert those who approach Jones Beach that they will not find desolate sandy wastes nor the unrelieved commercialism of an Atlantic City but rather a great public facility. Indeed Jones Beach today continues to be maintained by the Long Island State Park Region in a manner that would please Robert Moses, who long ago "promised the people on Long Island who gave us their beach land, that we would maintain certain standards." (RBM)

B

A: The Water Tower. B: West Bathhouse. C: Sign.
D: Jones Beach, 1933. E: Swimming pool,
West Bathhouse, in the thirties.

D

E

26

26. Henri Bendel / Walter P. Chrysler Estate (Now United States Merchant Marine Academy)

Steamboat Road, King's Point. Established on this site in 1943, the United States Merchant Marine Academy is a model of adaptive reuse of estate buildings and comprises, among a number of smaller structures, two former country estate houses. The Bendel / Chrysler estate, originally built in 1916 for Henri Bendel, the founder of the specialty store that bears his name, and owned by car manufacturer Walter P. Chrysler from 1923 to 1938, is now Wiley Hall, the administrative headquarters for the academy. This imposing white-stuccoed French Renaissance structure, designed by Henry Otis Chapman, Sr., is rectangular in form with restrained exterior detailing confined to quoins, balconets and a porte-cochere. The impressive axial main hall, open in the center to the second story, extends through the width of the house. Nearby, the Museum of the American Merchant Marine is housed in the former William S. Barstow estate, designed in 1930 for this noted inventor and former mayor of King's Point by New York City architect Greville Rickard in the Mediterranean Villa style. (CT)

27. "Ormston," John E. Aldred Estate (Now St. Josephat's Monastery)

Lattingtown Road and East Beach Road, Lattingtown (not open to the public). "Ormston," one of a small number of early twentieth-century Gold Coast estates that remain unsubdivided and relatively intact, was built in 1916 for John E. Aldred, a utility magnate and hydroelectric pioneer. In 1910 Aldred and his neighbor, lawyer W. D. Guthrie, bought 400 acres of land and demolished 60 houses to provide their adjoining estates with an uninterrupted view of Long Island Sound. Set amid 119 rolling and wooded acres, the estate was designed by Bertram Grosvenor Goodhue, architect of the Romanesque-Byzantine St. Bartholomew's Church in New York City. Although loosely based on sixteenth-century English Tudor country houses, the 74-room house represents, in its asymmetrical plan and pastiche of ornamentation, a purely twentieth-century American statement. Random-coursed fieldstone and limestone trim, gabled roofs, tall sculptural chimneys and windows of various types and sizes give the house its strong picturesque quality. Aldred lost his fortune and his estate in the early 1940s, and the building was sold in 1944 to the order of St. Basil the Great, a Ukrainian church. Today "Ormston" serves that order as St. Josephat's Monastery. (CT)

28. "Dormer House," Mrs. Charles O. Gates House

357 Lattingtown Road, Lattingtown (private residence—not open to the public). Theodate Pope Riddle, who designed this deep-roofed red-brick house in 1917, was one of the first woman architects in America. With talent, determination and her fortunate station in life, Pope cleared the obstacles confronting a Victorian woman who wanted to practice a traditionally male profession. Her first experience was restoring an eighteenth-century cottage for herself. Later she arranged tutoring from the art department at Princeton. Then, when her father hired Stanford White to build a house she had designed, she apprenticed herself to the most prestigious architectural firm working in New York. "Dormer House" is Pope's largest domestic project. The long, low house lies at the crest of a hill, its wings angled to conform to the land and trees on the site. A shingled roof of medieval steepness cascades down to the low walls, interrupted by a line of hipped dormers. The east wing was added in 1935. (EF)

27

28

Lattingtown

23

29

29. GELLER HOUSE

Ocean Avenue and Tanglewood Crossing, Lawrence (private residence — not open to the public). The nine-room Geller house of 1945, with its distinctive "butterfly" roof, has been called one of the most influential American houses of the 1940s. Architect Marcel Breuer referred to its layout as a "binuclear" plan with a central entry hall that separates living/dining areas from the private sleeping/study areas. Breuer also designed an adjacent guest house/garage building and was commissioned to design most of the furniture for the Geller family. Two of his other postwar houses on Long Island were the Tompkins House (1947) in Hewlett Harbor and the Hanson House (1951) on Lloyd's Neck. (AG)

30. R. A. PEABODY HOUSE

Ocean Avenue, Lawrence (private residence — not open to the public). This handsome Tudor Revival house stands in the Rockaway Hunt residential development laid out in the 1870s by the three Lawrence brothers, real-estate developers and speculators. The winding streets and naturalistic landscaping derive from Frederick Law Olmsted's interpretation of the English picturesque ideal popularized in the mid-nineteenth century. Designed by Renwick, Aspinwall & Owen, a New York firm descended from the great Gothic Revival architect James Renwick, the stucco and half-timber house is in the late Medieval Revival style that would soon become one of the most popular forms on America's suburban streets. The tall two-story and attic main block features asymmetrical gables connected by a steep-roofed center section that holds the great hall. The long lateral wing originally held the kitchen, servants' rooms and a laundry. (EF)

30

31

31. "ROCK HALL"

199 Broadway, Lawrence (open to the public: 239-1157). Preserving exceptional scale, architectural detailing and an orientation to the water, Rock Hall belongs to the tradition of the Caribbean "Great Houses" that were built for wealthy plantation owners throughout the eighteenth century. In fact, its existence on Long Island may be attributed to Josiah Martin, an Antiguan planter, who constructed the house in 1768 to oversee his mercantile interests in New York City. Martin was a loyalist, however, and suffered depredations during the Revolutionary War at the hands of patriotic Long Islanders before he died at "Rock Hall" in 1778. Thomas Hewlett, an ambitious local farmer, acquired the property from Martin's descendants in 1824. He may have been responsible for introducing Federal-period archways and other architectural features to the first floor during conversion of the house into a seasonal boardinghouse during the mid-nineteenth century. The Hewlett family later built the large east wing to accommodate modern systems in the 1880s, intentionally preserving the historic rooms unaltered. While much of the original acreage had been subdivided by the turn of the century, the Hewletts deeded the house to the Town of Hempstead in 1946 for museum purposes. "Rock Hall" is administered today by the town with curatorial assistance provided by the Society for the Preservation of Long Island Antiquities. (ZS) *31A: A Mathew Brady view of 1865.*

31A

Lawrence

32

33

32. LOCUST VALLEY FIREHOUSE

Buckram Road, Locust Valley. The Locust Valley Firehouse was designed in 1926 by Bradley Delehanty (1888–1965), an architect who established a successful practice in country house architecture on Long Island between the World Wars. As a summer resident of Locust Valley, Delehanty was the logical choice to design the new firehouse. While he designed in a great diversity of styles, traditional elements and classic proportions are evident in much of Delehanty's work, including this structure. The central mass of the Colonial style building rests on a beautifully proportioned Doric-columned first story and is crowned by a Chippendale-style second-story parapet and octagonal cupola. Formed in 1893, with its first truck house completed in 1898, the Locust Valley Fire Department has provided nearly 100 years of fire-fighting and community service. (CT)

33. LOCUST VALLEY JUNIOR HIGH SCHOOL

Bayville and Ryefield Roads, Locust Valley (Lattingtown). This architecturally significant public building was built in 1927 to plans supplied by Coffin & Coffin. The brick two-story structure has an octagonal tower with a belvedere over the center. The irregular mass contains two wings with administration, library, service and gymnasium facilities. Connecting the two wings are the classrooms. (CT)

34A

34. THE PIPING ROCK CLUB

Piping Rock Road, Locust Valley (private club — not open to the public). The Piping Rock Club was a late arrival among Long Island country clubs. Shinnecock (the first professionally designed golf course in America to be built in conjunction with a clubhouse), Rockaway, Meadowbrook, Nassau, Garden City, the National Golf Links and a number of other clubs were already well established by the time the Locust Valley club was completed in 1911. However, Piping Rock was to be precedent-setting in its facilities and architectural plan. Reminiscent of New York's Dutch Colonial architecture, the complex of shingled and porticoed forms reminded *Country Life* of "the sort of thing that George Washington would have built if he had the money."

Boston architect Guy Lowell brought unusual talents to bear on this commission. Educated in the 1890s at Harvard, MIT and the École des Beaux-Arts, he had also worked in the offices of landscape architect Édouard-François André while in Paris. By 1911 Lowell had designed such major buildings as Boston's Museum of Fine Arts, while establishing a reputation as a landscape architect

through commissions for Boston's Fenway and the publication of his book *American Gardens*. At Piping Rock, Lowell planned the building around an open courtyard making use of the internal hallway that surrounded it to access the ballroom, dining room, library and other club rooms. On the exterior, porches replete with awnings circled the structure. "Thus the building," as Marjorie Pearson has observed, "was placed into and linked with the landscape." Widely published in the decade following its completion, Piping Rock became a model among the second generation of country clubs, admired for both its novel plan and recreational facilities for pursuits that went well beyond golf to include polo, turf racing, horse shows and a variety of racket sports. The 1916 Doubleday travel novel *The Lightening Conductor Discovers America* called it an American Ranelagh and its influence was felt as far west as Chicago, where the Onwentsia Club at Lake Forest, Illinois, was based on its plan. (RBM) *34: The club in an antique photograph. 34A: As shown in an ad of the 1920s.*

35. JOSÉ LUIS SERT STUDIO/HOUSE

Locust Valley (private residence — not open to the public). The front part of this house is a two-story Modernist structure designed in 1951 to serve as the entrance link to the older, back part, originally a stable building that architect José Luis Sert remodeled but kept as a large open loftlike space (36′ × 75′, with a herringbone brick floor) for living, dining and kitchen purposes. "The room had to be brought together," wrote the architect, "and the furniture scaled to form part of the architecture. The different

pieces of furniture were designed to establish bridges or visual stepping stones between distant walls . . . The impression of big, uncluttered space had to be kept" (*Progressive Architecture*, August 1952). An open balcony above the garage was used by the architect as his studio. Sert, awarded the Gold Medal of the American Institute of Architects in 1981, established the first formal professional degree program in urban design in 1953 at Harvard, with which he was associated until 1969. (AG)

36. THE GRANADA TOWERS

310 Riverside Drive, Long Beach (private apartment house — can be seen from the road). Designed by the firm of Lang and Rosenberg as a luxury apartment house, the Granada Towers had the misfortune of being completed the week of the 1929 stock-market crash. Its subsequent history, according to local press accounts, has been one of "splendor, decay, and renewal." For a time abandoned, the National Register landmark was sym-

pathetically renovated for condominiums in the 1980s under the direction of Richard Bank, AIA The handsome Spanish Renaissance–inspired building is a reminder of the great 1920s Long Beach real-estate boom led by state Senator Reynolds, who attempted to create an American Riviera on the South Shore with Long Beach as New York's answer to Atlantic City. (RBM)

37. GLENDON ALLVINE HOUSE

Long Beach (private residence — not open to the public). Probably the first Modernist house on Long Island, if not the East Coast, the Allvine House was designed in 1929 by architect Warren Matthews. The stark white stucco building rose up unexpectedly, making a crisp angular incision into the low-lying dunescape of its Long Beach setting. Its black slate coping, setbacks, horizontal bands of windows, cantilevered sun decks and tubular metal railings were all borrowed from the preferred International Style. Its original interior furnishings were designed by top designers of

the day, such as Walter von Nessen, Donald Deskey, Ruth Reeves and Paul Frankl. All of it went together to make this innovative house something of a prototype for the essential Long Island modern beach house. With flat roofs, multilevel decks, open plan and large windows, it was a precedent of things to come. Its orientation toward the ocean and prowlike porch and series of porthole windows all reinforced the image of a futuristic ship about to set sail. (AG)

38. THE LIDO BEACH HOTEL

Richmond Road and Maple Boulevard, Long Beach (private apartment house — can be seen from the road). Last of the great resort hotels that once ringed Long Island, the Lido Beach opened in 1928, the four-million-dollar creation of Long Beach developer, State Senator William J. Reynolds. Schultze & Weaver, architects of the Waldorf-Astoria and "Montauk Manor" [*see* No. 182], designed the hotel in the then fashionable Spanish Renaissance style, a mode made popular by motion pictures and Florida's

new Gold Coast. The Lido's red-tile roof and huge minaret-like towers, said to be modeled on the Alhambra at Granada, did nothing to dissuade guests from the thought that they had arrived at a distant and romantic oasis. Amenities included an 18-hole golf course designed by Scotland's Blair MacDonald and a dance floor, covered by a retractable roof, where celebrity performers appeared. The five-story hotel was converted into condominiums in 1984. (RBM)

Locust Valley / Long Beach

37

38

39

40

Long Beach / Manhasset

30

39. LONG BEACH RAILROAD STATION

Park Avenue Station Plaza, Long Beach (open to the public). Built by the New York and Long Beach Railroad Co. in 1909, the 60′ × 120′ Spanish style depot on Park Avenue in Long Beach was the fanciful gateway to State Senator William J. Reynolds' great resort. One of a number of fine architect-designed stations of the resort era still in use by the Long Island Rail Road (including those at Glen Cove and Oakdale), the Long Beach facility's archi-tect was the Beaux-Arts–trained Kenneth M. Murchison (1872–1938), who specialized in railroad stations and counted among his commissions Baltimore's Union Railroad Station. The noted land-scape architect Charles Wellford Leavitt (1871–1928) also was involved in planning the terminus, which in 1962 appeared in the film *That Kind of Woman*, starring Sophia Loren. (RBM)

40. "INISFADA," NICHOLAS F. BRADY ESTATE (NOW SAINT IGNATIUS RETREAT HOUSE)

Searingtown Road, Manhasset (private retreat house — not open to the public). "Inisfada," Gaelic for Long Island, is set in a thickly wooded landscape, the imposing house emerging from a small rise. Built between 1916 and 1920 for one of the foremost Catholic lay couples in the United States, utilities executive Nicholas F. Brady and his wife, Genevieve Garvan Brady, "Inis-fada" has had a history highlighted by the visit of Cardinal Eugenio Pacelli, later Pope Pius XII, in 1936. In 1937 Mrs. Brady donated the estate to the New York Province of the Society of Jesus and it now serves as a Jesuit retreat house. The only Long Island work of the Philadelphia architect John Torrey Windrim (1866–1934), "Inisfada," faced with brick and trimmed in dressed limestone, is a lively interpretation of the Tudor–Elizabethan Revival style. Quoining, crenelations and battlements, interspersed with grouped square-headed, stone-mullioned windows, create a pic-turesque facade, while the gables, roofed in gray slate, and 33 Tudor chimneys (none alike) emphasize the vertical thrust of the composition. Although the present owners have removed much of the interior appointments, creating an environment more in keep-ing with their ascetic ideals, some of the original oak paneling, Jacobean strapwork and ribbed plaster ceilings survive. (CT)

41. HEWLETT–MUNSON HOUSE

200 Port Washington Boulevard, Manhasset (private residence — not open to the public). One of the many Long Island houses associated with the prolific Hewlett family is this large center-hall dwelling. The area itself is historically linked to the seventeenth-century Hempstead settlement, having served as grazing land used in raising livestock, an occupation which George Hewlett (1634–1722) is documented to have pursued. Hewlett assembled a considerable estate on Cow Neck, as it was then called, and built houses there for his sons Samuel and James in the early eighteenth century. A single room within the present structure may date to 1675, establishing the Hewlett–Munson House as an early "hovel" dating from Cow Neck's first period of settlement. Enlargement of the house took place in later centuries, the most recent accretion being a turn-of-the-century wing at-tached by Carlos W. Munson, owner of the Munson Steamship Line. After Munson's death in 1940 much of the estate was ac-quired by Levitt and Sons for development, while the old house has been preserved and maintained by a sympathetic owner. (ZS)

Planned Communities

A

B

C

*F*rom the creation of Brooklyn Heights, "the first suburb," following the establishment of regular ferry service from Manhattan in 1814, Long Island has been a cradle of suburbanization and a testing ground for planned communities. Lured by its temperate climate, inviting topography and progressive transportation improvements, the visionary, the utopian and the practical looked to the advantages of Long Island.

The communities that they created include some of the most celebrated Anglo-American planned suburbs of the last hundred and fifty years. Garden City (1869), department store magnate A.T. Stewart's model village for his employees, may have even had its name borrowed by the famous English planner Ebenezer Howard for his idealized town plan *Garden Cities Of Tomorrow* (1902). Forest Hills Gardens (1912), designed for the Russell Sage Foundation as a model village of lower income housing by Grosvenor Atterbury with the Olmsted Brothers as landscape architects, and Sunnyside Gardens (1924) are known internationally. The most famous of all, however, is the community that epitomized post–World War II suburban development, Levittown.

Between 1947 and 1951 the Levitts were to build 17,447 houses utilizing assembly-line procedures and slab construction (concrete slabs embedded with radiant heating coils were used in place of basements) which initially retailed for $6,990. Yet Levittown represented more than just affordable housing, for the Levitts built playgrounds, swimming pools, village greens, a baseball field and a community center, while planting over half a million trees. As it nears its fiftieth anniversary in the 1990s, America's first great postwar new town has survived its critics (such as Lewis Mumford, who feared the nearly identical housing and same-generation ownership would create an instant slum), and the Levitts are recognized as the housing industry's twentieth-century equivalent to Henry Ford.

Scholars are now focusing on the Levitts' early projects, their upper income level subdivisions of the 1930s (all called Strathmore) which were located at Rockville Centre, Manhasset and Great Neck. Strathmore–Vanderbilt (1938), one of three projects by the Levitts in Manhasset, was built on the former 115-acre Sherry–Munsey–Vanderbilt Estate and is of particular interest because the amenities included a resident-owned clubhouse (the former mansion), recreational facilities and a "necessities building."

A: Levittown. B: Subdivision map of Munsey Park.
C: The Strathmores, North Strathmore, Manhasset.
D: Stores and post office, Stony Brook Village Center.
E: Belle Terre Country Club (demolished). F: Typical Belle Terre residence. G: Aerial View of Stony Brook Village Center.

Other examples in Nassau and Suffolk counties of early planned communities include Belle Terre (1902 and after), east of Port Jefferson, a "club colony" of upper and middle income housing developed by Dean Alvord. Alvord and his architect, John J. Petit, fresh from the success of their parklike Prospect Park South development in Brooklyn, created a self-contained resort community replete with a clubhouse, golf course and sixty miles of landscaped roads and bridle trails which were accessed by a handsome new Port Jefferson railroad terminal which they built in 1903. Contemporary with Belle Terre was "Sugar King" H. O. Havemeyer's Moorish style community of Bayberry Point at Islip [*see* No. 160], tobacco magnate Benjamin Duke's Spanish-themed Plandome Heights (1909) and Thomas Benton Ackerson's Brightwaters (1907), a seaside development boasting lakes, a yacht harbor and beach casino.

Planned "park" developments of the 1920s and 1930s included University Gardens (1927) in Great Neck, Beacon Hill at Port Washington and Munsey Park (1928) in Manhasset, which was developed for the Metropolitan Museum with strict architectural controls, deed restrictions and streets named for famous American artists. Thom McAn shoe king Ward Melville's community-wide business and philanthropic projects around Stony Brook, both before and after the war, are also noteworthy. Melville's reconstruction of the village's business center resulted in one of the region's first auto accessed shopping centers (1940–41), dozens of amenities running the gamut from horse show grounds to a museum and half a dozen subdivisions, starting with Old Field South in 1929. The vast majority of these buildings were designed in the Colonial Revival manner by one architect, Richard H. Smythe, a college classmate whose work for Melville spanned four decades and included hundreds of commissions. (RBM)

E

F

D

G

42

42. HORATIO G. ONDERDONK HOUSE

1471 Northern Boulevard, Manhasset. Unlike the modest and familiar farmhouses built in the vicinity, Judge Horatio G. Onderdonk's Greek Revival 1836 country seat bespoke the builder's affluence and sophistication. Not attributed to any architect or builder's guide, this stylish house nevertheless employs the plan and exterior detailing of a formal house type that began to appear with some frequency by the mid-1830s. Its imposing two-story columns support a low-pitched pediment, while the one-story wings and upper roof are an early example of tin roofing on Long Island. The judge's law office, a diminutive single-room "mini-temple" that once stood on the front lawn, was apparently demolished in the 1930s when the house served as a construction office for the noted developers Levitt and Sons. Now the property of The Strathmore Association, the house is accessible for community groups and educational purposes. (ZS)

43. JOHN HAY WHITNEY BOATHOUSE

26 Lake Road, Manhasset (private residence — not open to the public). Boathouses are rare on Long Island's North Shore because of a six-foot tide fall, but then the central bay of John Hay Whitney's 1929 boathouse at Manhasset Bay was not actually a boatwell but rather a space in which to house an amphibious plane with a forty-foot wingspan. Designed by C. Grant La Farge (1862–1938), son of the famous artist John La Farge and architect of J. P. Morgan's Glen Cove mansion (now demolished) and Theodore Roosevelt's 1905 addition to "Sagamore Hill," the jerkin-head-roofed Arts and Crafts–inspired boathouse is clad in red-cedar shingles above a random ashlar basement. Stone is also employed at both ends of the transverse gable and above the plane bay. A club room with a recessed porch, bedrooms and bar were decorated by La Farge in the Moderne mode with exposed beams and nautical-rope moldings. (RBM)

44. "THE CLIFFS," JAMES W. BEEKMAN HOUSE

West Shore Road, Mill Neck (private residence — not open to the public). Arguably the first mansion of the "great estate phenomenon" on Long Island, which spanned the period between the Civil War and Pearl Harbor, James W. Beekman's "The Cliffs" (1863–64) rose while the Civil War hostilities still raged. The picturesquely massed Gothic Revival house, with its welter of paneled chimneys and steep gables framing Gothic and rosette windows, is reminiscent of a mid-Victorian Hudson River villa. Its architect, the English émigré Henry G. Harrison (1813–1895), specialized in ecclesiastical work and later designed the Cathedral of the Incarnation at Garden City. Beekman, scion of a prominent Manhattan family and a civic leader who had served in the New York State Senate, was interested in horticulture and had supported the creation of Central Park. The romantically landscaped grounds of his country house, laid out in accordance with the principles of the landscape architect Andrew Jackson Downing, with whom Beekman had worked a decade before on establishing Central Park, became one of the showplaces of Oyster Bay's nascent summer colony. By the turn of the century, the Beekmans had established a remarkable series of gardens including "the Big Flower Garden," the "Water Gardens," the "Croton Garden" and the "Alma-Tadema Pool Garden." (RBM)

43

44

Manhasset / Mill Neck

35

45

45. "SEFTON MANOR" (NOW MILL NECK SCHOOL FOR THE DEAF)

Frost Mill Road, Mill Neck (private school — not open to the public). "Sefton Manor," with its oak-paneled rooms, carved-stone chimneypieces, Elizabethan-inspired molded-plaster ceilings and stained-glass windows illustrating scenes from Shakespeare's plays, is a fine example of the twentieth-century American revival of English Tudor design. The exterior's symmetrical main block is composed of light brown Westchester granite, coped and trimmed with limestone, its west facade inspired by St. Catherine's Court, Somersetshire, England. Built in 1923 by Lillian Sefton Thomas Dodge, who was the president of the Harriet Hubbard Ayer Co., the cosmetics firm founded in 1907 by her first husband, Vincent B. Thomas, the estate was sold in 1949 to the Mill Neck Manor School for the Deaf. The house was designed by Clinton & Russell, Wells, Holton & George, a firm formed in 1894 with the partnership of Clinton, who apprenticed in the office of Richard Upjohn, architect of New York's Trinity Church, and Russell, who had studied with his famous uncle, James Renwick, designer of St. Patrick's Cathedral. (CT)

46. "MARGROVE," GROVER LOENING HOUSE

Horseshoe Road, Mill Neck (private residence — not open to the public). In 1930 Grover Loening, an aeronautical engineer, designed his own Mill Neck residence. Said to be completed by airplane mechanics from Loening's factory, the Modernistic "Margrove" is characterized by its horizontality and smooth wall surface, comprised of brick with an American Indian motif woven into the parapet design. The interior, awash in the iconography of flight, features frescoes of the sky and railings constructed of aeronautical steel alloy with an abstract seagull design expressive of motion. (CT) *46: Interior with staircase. 46A: Exterior view.*

46

47. "OAK KNOLL," BERTRAM G. WORK HOUSE

Cleft Road, Mill Neck (private residence — not open to the public). Delano & Aldrich, whose partnership branched out of the Carrère & Hastings office in 1903, experienced its greatest success in designing opulent country estates. The firm's trademark, architectural understatement and refinement, is apparent in "Oak Knoll," the austere Palladian-style villa built in 1916 for lawyer Bertram Work. Set on a ridge overlooking Oyster Bay, the estate lays a formal pattern over the woodland: beyond iron gates, at the end of a winding drive, a paved forecourt sets off the stuccoed entrance front, with a porch in an exedra screened by a curved portico. Around the house, formal gardens, a terrace and a fountain pool organize the landscape, with other, more secret gardens and service complexes tucked away in clearings in the woods. (EF)

46A

47

Mill Neck

37

48

49

48. NASSAU COUNTY COURTHOUSE

Franklin Avenue, Mineola (open to the public). On a warm Friday in July 1900, Governor Theodore Roosevelt congratulated the citizens of Nassau County on the new courthouse beginning to rise in Mineola. (Nassau had split off from Queens in 1898, when the western part of the old county joined Greater New York.) William Bunker Tubby's building is a stately Renaissance Revival design, centered on a monumental porticoed pavilion with a tall dome reminiscent of the Capitol in Washington. Tubby, originally a Brooklyn architect, specialized in row houses, mansions and public buildings. When his prominent clients began building Long Island summer houses around the turn of the century, Tubby followed them, extending his practice eastward. (EF)

49. "WHITE EAGLE," DU PONT–GUEST ESTATE
(NOW DE SEVERSKY CONFERENCE CENTER OF THE NEW YORK INSTITUTE OF TECHNOLOGY)

Northern Boulevard, Old Westbury. Thomas Hastings (design partner of Carrère & Hastings) fashioned "White Eagle" for Alfred I. du Pont right after a family quarrel spurred du Pont's relocation from Delaware to New York City. The red-brick mansion, built in 1916–17, spreads under broad hipped roofs, blending Georgian and Adam Neoclassicism with a dash of Renaissance drama. In the Beaux-Arts manner, the house originally focused the landscape around it. The front (south) entry, emphasized by a monumental paired-column portico, ran through the house to open on terraced gardens full of water features. In the mid-1920s, Mrs. Frederick E. Guest (daughter of Andrew Carnegie's partner Henry Phipps) bought the estate, renaming it "Templeton." After her death, it was acquired by NYIT and is presently used as a conference center. (EF)

50

50. "KNOLE," DURYEA–MARTIN HOUSE

Wheatley Road, Old Westbury (private residence—not open to the public). Carrère & Hastings, Beaux-Arts trained architects in partnership since 1885, burst into prominence with the New York Public Library, begun in 1902. Design partner Thomas Hastings practiced the French architectural philosophy, which emphasized the comprehensive planning of every element of an estate, from mansion and landscape to vistas. "Knole," built for Herman B. Duryea in 1903, tops a small hill. Its restrained, Palladian entrance facade in gleaming white stucco is countered by exuberant classicism at the garden front behind. A magnificent elliptical rotunda focuses the 40-room house, which opens onto a formal water garden with walks and woods beyond. The 33-acre estate (still a private residence) includes eighteenth- and nineteenth-century buildings on its grounds, and Carrère & Hastings added an indoor tennis court in 1921. (EF) *50: The garden courtyard, 1906. 50A: The west facade.*

50A

51

51. A. Conger Goodyear House

Wheatley Road, Old Westbury (private residence — not open to the public). While the basic look of this 1938 house, with its flat roof and floor-to-ceiling glass walls, evokes the spirit of European Modernism, architect Edward Durell Stone (1902–1978) broke with strict International Style dogma by using deep roof overhangs to block out the harmful rays of the summer sun. To house the original owner's collection of important modern art, Stone designed a central gallery space as the "spinal column" around which all the other rooms project. The main living room is circular in plan, with its southern side all glass, opening out to expansive views of the surrounding landscape. Stone, an exponent in his later work of the New Formalism, designed the United States Pavilion at the Brussels World's Fair (1958). (AG)

52. Isaac Hicks House

Jericho Turnpike, Old Westbury (private residence — not open to the public). The Isaac Hicks house, a vernacular Greek Revival design combining several later additions, is situated on its original site. Built ca. 1835 by Isaac Hicks, it descended in the family for nearly a century and a half until its acquisition for restoration and resale with preservation restrictions by the Society for the Preservation of Long Island Antiquities in 1979. The builder was a son of Elias Hicks, a prominent and outspoken Quaker who founded the so-called "Hicksite" branch of the society that remains active on Long Island, in New York and New England. Elias died in 1830, leaving a large family that was successful in many occupations across Long Island throughout the nineteenth century. Isaac Hicks & Sons became a leading commercial nursery in the 1860s and a portion of the extensive farms that surround the Hicks house remain under cultivation to this day. The farmhouse preserves its conservative three-bay, two-story main block as well as a kitchen wing now enlarged with an upper story. Interior detailing such as the hall staircase, parlor doors and mantelpieces, and decorative plasterwork are all intact from the construction period. (ZS)

52

Old Westbury

53. "WESTBURY HOUSE," JOHN S. PHIPPS ESTATE (NOW OLD WESTBURY GARDENS)

71 Old Westbury Road, Old Westbury (open to the public: 333-0048). Evocative of stately eighteenth-century English Georgian houses, "Westbury House" was designed in 1906 by an English architect, George A. Crawley, with American architects Alfred C. Bossom, Edward Hinkle and Grosvenor Atterbury as Stateside collaborators. In 1911 a wing was designed by Philadelphia architect Horace Trumbauer. The two-and-a-half-story Neo-Georgian structure, laid out along an east–west axis, has identical pavilions projecting on either side of the rectangular main body. The red-brick and limestone trim of the facade contrasts delicately with the broad hipped roof of yellow slate, while dominating the center of the roof is a two-story chimney stack spanned by a round arch. Built for John S. Phipps — son of Henry Phipps, financier and partner in the Carnegie Steel Company — and his English bride, Margarita C. Grace, Westbury House is one of the few remaining estates to retain its original furnishings. The grounds of the estate, also designed by Crawley, contain over 70 beautifully landscaped acres influenced by elements of both English Romantic and French Renaissance landscape design, including the Walled Garden, the Lilac Walk and the formal Rose Gardens. Old Westbury Gardens is open to the public as a museum and arboretum. (CT) *53: Garden facade. 53A: Front facade.*

54

55

54. ADAM–DERBY HOUSE

166 Lexington Avenue, Oyster Bay (private residence — not open to the public). In 1878, following the death of her husband, the president of the New York Gas Light Company, Sarah Sampson Adam decided to return to her native Oyster Bay and build a new house on the property she had inherited from her father, Isaac Sampson. Mantels, doors and interior trim, recycled from Isaac's Greek Revival domicile, which had been razed to make way for the new structure, can still be seen on the second floor of the house, but that was the only economy Sarah allowed herself in commissioning a spectacular Shingle Style mansion, designed by the distinguished firm of Potter & Robertson. Discussed by architectural historian Vincent J. Scully, Jr. in his landmark study on the Shingle Style, the Adam–Derby house is noteworthy for its exterior appearance and early use of English Queen Anne detailing, as seen in its half-timbering and sunflower decorations. Long the home of Theodore Roosevelt's youngest daughter Ethel and her husband Dr. Richard N. Derby, who occupied the house from 1913 until Mrs. Derby's death in 1977, the Adam–Derby house is now the centerpiece of a town-house development known as Landmark Colony at Oyster Bay. (RBM)

55. "COE HALL," WILLIAM ROBERTSON COE ESTATE (NOW PLANTING FIELDS ARBORETUM)

Planting Fields Road, Oyster Bay (open to the public: 922-9200). "Coe Hall," the centerpiece of a grandly conceived 350-acre estate named "Planting Fields," was the product of the 40-year award-winning architectural partnership of Walker & Gillette. The Neo-Tudor main residence, incorporating medieval and Elizabethan details, features oriel windows, gabled dormers, clusters of tall, highly decorative chimneys and a facade of half-timbering combined with pale Indiana limestone. Built in 1918 for English-born William Robertson Coe and his wife Mai Rogers (daughter of Henry Huddleston Rogers, a founder of Standard Oil), "Planting Fields" evolved into the horticultural showplace it is today thanks to the Coes' interest in rare species and plant collection. Landscape advisers for the estate included such prestigious names in the field of landscape design as Guy Lowell, A. Robeson Sargent and the Olmsted Brothers. A unique feature of the estate, now a museum open to the public, is the Carshalton Gates, wrought in 1712 for Carshalton Park, an English country house, and purchased by Coe in 1921 — the 113-foot span is considered to be one of the finest extant examples of English eighteenth-century wrought-iron and repoussé work. (CT)

56. "MALLOW," WALTER FARWELL HOUSE (NOW EAST WOODS SCHOOL)

31 Yellowcote Road, Oyster Bay (private school — not open to the public). The elegant Georgian Revival "Mallow" was designed in 1918 for Chicago-born financier Walter Farwell by William Welles Bosworth. Bosworth trained at MIT, then at the École des Beaux-Arts, and worked in the offices of Henry Hobson Richardson, Carrère & Hastings and Frederick Law Olmsted. He toured Europe with the Georgian Revivalist William Rotch Ware. From his experience, Bosworth was persuaded to "stick to the Greeks' concept of beauty for life," and he worked in the classical tradition with versatility and an elegance of touch that is apparent in this 26-room residence. The two-story brick house has a nine-bay entrance front articulated by full-height pilasters supporting a brick-and-wood baluster parapet that screens a low-hipped roof. The garden front, which opens on formal terraces, garden and pool, features the two-story semioctagonal bay that houses the tall salon. Now the home of the East Woods School, the building has been sympathetically adapted for its current use. (EF)

57

57. FIRST PRESBYTERIAN CHURCH

East Main Street, Oyster Bay (open to the public). The Stick Style of the 1870s, a movement in architectural "truthfulness" characterized by the exterior expression of a building's frame through the use of vertical boarding, sharp angles and large brackets, is recalled on Long Island by Oyster Bay's First Presbyterian Church. Designed by the architect J. C. Cady (1837–1919), who also designed many other institutional and ecclesiastical structures, the 1873 house of worship exhibits such classic features of the style as board-and-batten siding, exposed trusses and framing, and a steeple that explodes into a basketry of "stickwork." Even the steeple roof expresses the unseen frame beneath it. The original polychromatic Victorian paint scheme would have further accentuated the vertical elements. (RBM)

58. FREDERICK LUTZ HOUSE

Yellowcote Road, Oyster Bay (private residence — not open to the public). Harrie T. Lindeberg, practicing on his own after the dissolution of his partnership with Lewis Albro, designed this English-style cottage for Frederick Lutz in 1917. In both picturesque restraint and concern for the "entourage" (natural and architectural setting), Lindeberg's work here and elsewhere is reminiscent of that of the influential pre–World War I country house designer Sir Edwin Lutyens. Several of Lindeberg's trademark features appear in the Lutz house: the richly textured wood-shingle roof, the warm-hued stucco facade, the broad windows — often set in pairs and clusters — and the vine-covered pergolas that cast shifting patterns of light and shade over the surface of the house. Lindeberg allowed his houses the most advanced technologies to make them solid and comfortable, but their finish and handmade ornament demonstrate his affinity with the Arts and Crafts movement. (EF)

59. "RAYNHAM HALL"

West Main Street, Oyster Bay Hamlet (open to the public: 922-6808). Benedict Arnold's treachery was discovered through conversations overheard at "Raynham Hall" when British officers were billeted here during the American Revolution. The eavesdropper, Sally Townsend, sent word to her brother Robert, alias "Culper, Jr.," an agent of General Washington's intelligence service. The Townsend family seat from 1738 to 1941, "Raynham Hall" today reflects the results of two distinct building campaigns. The eighteenth-century, five-bay, center-hall saltbox visible from West Main Street contrasts sharply with the two-story Victorian addition at the rear. This nineteenth-century modernization included "Victorianizing" the older part of the structure with an offset tower, porte-cochere and decorative elements, all since removed. Deeded to the Town of Oyster Bay in 1947, "Raynham Hall" is operated as a house museum by the Friends of Raynham Hall. (KB)

58

59

60

60. "SAGAMORE HILL," THEODORE ROOSEVELT HOUSE

Cove Neck Road, Oyster Bay (museum — open to the public).
In 1884, Theodore Roosevelt, soon to be the country's twenty-sixth president, commissioned New York architects Lamb & Rich to design a country house in Oyster Bay, with which T. R. had long been familiar, having spent summer childhoods there as a boy. The area's natural resources for fishing, hiking and boating, combined with its newly formed summer colony, created the ideal environment for the active, athletic and sociable statesman. The multigabled Queen Anne house, solid and substantial with generous verandas, was enlivened by its exuberant exterior detailing. Stone and brick were used for the first story and cedar shingles, in both wave and fish-scale patterns, for the second story, painted in a polychromatic scheme of red, ocher and yellow. Lamb & Rich, the designers of several other country residences on Long Island, were also known for their educational buildings, such as Pratt Institute (1887), and for pioneering in the development of low-cost apartment houses, including the Astral Apartment Building in Brooklyn (1886). Named after a Long Island Indian chief, "Sagamore Hill" acted as the President's summer White House, with the 1905 North Room addition, designed by Christopher Grant La Farge, functioning as a presidential reception room. "Sagamore Hill" is now operated as a National Historic Site administered by the National Park Service. (CT)

61. "YELLOWBANKS," JAMES A. ROOSEVELT HOUSE

Cove Neck Road, Oyster Bay (private residence — not open to the public). Bruce Price, a late nineteenth-century architect of national reputation, whose use of space and mass are believed to have influenced Frank Lloyd Wright, designed "Yellowbanks," his only Long Island domestic commission, in 1881. The Shingle Style house derives its name from the forsythia that line the bank on which it is situated overlooking Oyster Bay. Price's client, James Alfred Roosevelt, an astute businessman who transformed his family's plate-glass business into Roosevelt & Son, an investment banking firm, was T. R.'s uncle. With its gambrel roof and shingle work, "Yellowbanks" presages the appearance of the Colonial Revival style. Still privately owned, the house can only be seen from the water. (RBM)

62. "THE EVERGREENS," EDWARD H. SWAN HOUSE

Cove Neck Road, Oyster Bay (private residence — not open to the public). "The Evergreens," the Edward H. Swan House in the Incorporated Village of Cove Neck, was one of the first architect-designed country houses on Long Island. It is also among the region's finest examples of the French Second Empire Style, which flourished during General Grant's presidency and had as its hallmark the mansard roof. The rage in Paris during the third quarter of the nineteenth century, the style took its name from the reign of Napoleon III (1852–70), which was known as the Second Empire. The house's architect, John W. Ritch (b. 1822), who trained in the offices of William Hurry and designed banks, hospitals and domiciles during a long career that extended into the 1890s, owed his commission to a fire. An earlier house on the site, designed by Ritch for Swan, was destroyed in a conflagration in 1858, soon after its completion. The event so disturbed Edward's father, a prominent New York shipowner and merchant, that he financed the construction of a new fire-resistant masonry villa for his son in 1872 with a slate roof and cast-iron porches. With its tripartite facade, projecting central pavilion, round-headed windows and mansard roof, Edward's fashionable residence became one of the first showplaces of Oyster Bay's summer colony. The young Theodore Roosevelt was to teach Edward's daughter Emily the "new game" of lawn tennis here in 1879. "The Evergreens" was listed on the National Register of Historic Places in 1976 and Ritch's specifications for the house survive in the collection of the Society for the Preservation of Long Island Antiquities. (RBM)

61

62

OLD BETHPAGE VILLAGE RESTORATION

Round Swamp Road, Old Bethpage
museum — open to the public / 420-5280

*O*ld Bethpage Village Restoration was initiated in 1962 to interpret nineteenth-century rural Long Island and enable preservation of a significant number of historic Long Island buildings that were disappearing rapidly because of suburban growth. Architecturally distinguished examples of Long Island's vernacular style have been a primary determinant in building selection. The majority of village buildings represent the American and English folk tradition, derived from New England, that continued from the seventeenth to the nineteenth centuries. An early variant is the Schenck House, with its eighteenth-century flared eaves and massive beams representing the Dutch influence on Long Island.

Many houses illustrate the popular massed two-story country Georgian style and the later Federal symmetrical style — from the gambrel-roofed eighteenth-century Lawrence House up to the mid nineteenth-century Noon Inn. The one-story Benjamin House (1829) represents the Cape Cod influence on the North Fork of Long Island. In the early 1800s, the fervor for classical themes spread on Long Island, although not with the intensity of elsewhere. Simple Greek Revival elements, such as the wide entablature, porches and columns of the Manetto Church and Kirby House, provide stylistic contrast.

A complete departure by mid-century is evident in the romantic and exuberant Gothic lines of the Coles House, representing the style contemporary with the Civil War.

The mixture of house styles is complemented by a wide variety of English barn forms, carriage houses, smoke- and outhouses, blacksmith's and hatmaker's shops and other utilitarian structures that evidence our folk architecture.

The 62 buildings at Old Bethpage represent an outdoor museum of Long Island architecture from 1740 to 1870. Part of the Nassau County Historical Museum, Old Bethpage Village Restoration is open year-round. (EJS)

A: Schenck House. B: Manetto Church.
C: Luyster Store. D: Kirby House.

B

C

A

D

63. St. Margaret's Episcopal Church

1000 Washington Avenue, Plainview (open to the public). The openwork bell tower and board-and-batten siding of St. Margaret's Episcopal Church in Plainview appear to be a contemporary interpretation of the Stick Style of the 1870s. Built in 1964 as a memorial to Margaret Shattuck on land donated by her husband Edward, the church has an interior that is also noteworthy, with exposed wooden trusses and triangular stained-glass windows. St. Margaret's Manhattan-based architect, Edward W. Slater, is no stranger to ecclesiastical architecture, having designed many houses of worship on Long Island, including the Neo-Expressionist Trinity Evangelical Lutheran Church at Rocky Point. (RBM) *63A: The architect's elevation.*

64. Dodge Homestead

58 Harbor Road, Port Washington (private residence — not open to the public). The one-and-one-half-story, five-bay Dodge Homestead, with stone cellar and lean-to addition, has the distinction of being one of Nassau County's earliest buildings. Located on the Mill Pond on Cow Neck Peninsula, it was built ca. 1721 by Thomas Dodge and inhabited by seven generations of his descendants. Originally known as Dodge's Inlet, the Pond was first harnessed for power ca. 1750 by Cock's Mill. The year 1795 saw the damming of the inlet, leading to the construction of new mills for grinding grain, spinning wool and cutting lumber. A weaver by trade, Dodge made cloth from materials produced at these mills. In 1750 Dodge expanded the house by adding a kitchen, a dining room and a weaving room. (KB)

65.

65. "VILLA CAROLA," ISAAC GUGGENHEIM ESTATE
(NOW THE IBM MANAGEMENT TRAINING CENTER)

Middle Neck Road, Port Washington (private — not open to the public). Of the seven sons of mining magnate Meyer Guggenheim, Isaac Guggenheim and two of his brothers selected Long Island sites for their country estates. Isaac chose the talented architect, artist and sculptor H. Van Buren Magonigle (1867–1935) to design the main house (1916) as well as a private golf clubhouse on the property (1922). Magonigle received his early training in the offices of Vaux & Bradford and later McKim, Mead & White, and began his own practice in 1909. Although faced in brick, "Villa Carola" in form and detail recalls an Italian villa with its tiled hip roof, wide overhanging eaves and large square tower. The house surrounds three sides of a courtyard, the garden facade having two symmetrical wings projecting from a recessed central block. A variety of window treatments enlivens the composition. With Isaac's death in 1922 the estate passed to his brother Solomon. In the 1970s "Villa Carola" became the IBM Management Training Center. (CT)

66. MAIN STREET SCHOOL

Main Street and South Washington Street, Port Washington. The Main Street School is a distinguished, monumentally scaled example of early twentieth-century Georgian Revival architecture. The imposing four-story building, prominently situated on the crest of a hill overlooking Manhasset Harbor, serves as the community's most prominent civic and architectural landmark, a designated town landmark that was nominated to the National Register in 1983. Built during the period of Beaux-Arts influence and completed in 1909, the rectangular structure is made of brick and is dramatically enlivened by bold stone quoining. The steep gable roof is dominated by an ornamental cupola with four clock faces. The plans for the school were accepted from two local architects, Frank Cornell and Ralph Dusinberre. Cornell was also the architect of other community buildings in the area, including the North Hempstead Town Hall, the Port Washington Post Office and the Huntington Public School. In 1917 an addition, also designed by Cornell, was made to the Main Street School's north elevation. (CT)

67. PORT WASHINGTON PUBLIC LIBRARY

249 Main Street, Port Washington (open to the public). The concrete-and-glass learning center at 249 Main Street in Port Washington is one of Long Island's most acclaimed new libraries. Designed by Curtis and Davis, the split-level structure, built between 1968 and 1970, is arranged with the entrance lobby and circulation desks at mid-level and the major public spaces just a half-level away. Well-connected to both its parking area and Main Street, the exterior is noteworthy for its unusual massing, in which the architects sought to conform to a sloping site and avoid an appearance of monumentality. By successfully juxtaposing elements, Curtis and Davis created an interesting play of light and shadow while board-forming the granite-toned concrete to replicate a wood-grain finish. (RBM)

66

67

Port Washington

51

68

69

68. "Homewood," Sands–Willets House (now Cow Neck Peninsula Historical Society)

336 Port Washington Boulevard, Port Washington (museum — open to the public). Now the headquarters of the Cow Neck Peninsula Historical Society, the Sands–Willets House is historically associated with two prominent Port Washington families. Generations of the Sands family, who gave their name to Sands Point, occupied a one-and-a-half-story eighteenth-century house, which now forms the west wing. Title passed in 1846 from Elizabeth G. Sands to Edmund Willets, a New York merchant, who is credited with enlarging the house in the Greek Revival style shortly thereafter. Descendants owned the property until 1965. Now a museum, both the house and a restored Dutch barn are open to the public. (ZS)

69. St. Agnes Cathedral

Clinton Avenue and College Place, Rockville Centre (open to the public). In the summer of 1887, the Catholics of Rockville Centre celebrated the first Mass in their town in a blacksmith's shop on Centre Avenue. After years of worshipping in adapted buildings, the parish completed its first church, a small Romanesque Revival building in rock-faced white marble, in 1905. That same year, Father Peter Quealy — an immigrant who had arrived from Ireland during the blizzard of 1888 — was named master builder to the parish. One by one, a complex of church structures — schools, a rectory and a convent — began to rise on church land at the corner of Clinton Avenue and College Place. The last and the greatest of them, the cathedral itself, was begun in 1933 and dedicated in October 1935. The Norman-Gothic style church, of limestone-trimmed buff brick with a single cross-crowned tower, became a cathedral in 1957 with the formation of the Diocese of Rockville Centre. The interior was modernized for practical and liturgical purposes in 1981–82, but the exterior, complete with the anvil from the 1887 blacksmith's shop, is in its original condition. (EF)

70. James K. Davis House

139 East Broadway, Roslyn (private residence — not open to the public). James K. Davis, the foremost contractor-builder in Roslyn during the late nineteenth century, was associated with such buildings as the Bryce–Frick estate and Clarence Mackay's "Harbor Hill" (demolished). The house he built for himself in 1877 combined elements of the Italianate and Second Empire styles, best described as "Victorian Eclectic." The second story supports a slated mansard roof capped with a delicate cast-iron cresting. The most important feature of the house is a square Italianate tower projecting a full story above the mansard. The windows provide much of the architectural character of the house, either trimmed with ogee molding or with pointed upper sashes set in pairs in gable-roofed dormers. The interior of the house is typical of both its styles. The original "front rooms" had plaster-ceiling cornices and chandelier medallions and marbleized slate mantels in the Rococo Revival style. The Davis house has descended with little subsequent alteration and is now undergoing refurbishing by new owners. (RGG)

70

71

71. "CLIFTON"

355 Bryant Avenue, Roslyn Harbor (private residence — not open to the public). Situated on the west bank of Hempstead Harbor, "Clifton" was built by Mrs. William (Ann Eliza) Cairns in 1863 after designs by Frederick S. Copley. A two-and-a-half-story structure with Flemish gable ends (an extremely unusual feature in England as well as America), the house was originally sheathed with flush-boarding to give the appearance of stone. The house had a steeply pitched slate roof, which has survived, and an elaborate Tudor-arched porch on all but the north front. In autumn 1920,

Mr. and Mrs. John N. Demarest, who occupied the house between 1917 and 1932, invited General John J. Pershing, Commander-in-Chief of the American Expeditionary Forces during World War I, to spend a few months at "Sycamore Lodge," as it was then called. Local residents still recall the sentry boxes at each gate during General Pershing's residence, as well as flag-raising ceremonies on the north lawn. "Clifton" has been altered significantly on its south end, but otherwise remains much the same as when it was built. (RGG)

72 & 73. "CEDARMERE" AND GOTHIC MILL, WILLIAM CULLEN BRYANT RESIDENCE

Bryant Avenue, Roslyn Harbor (museum — currently in the process of restoration). "Cedarmere" was the home of William Cullen Bryant, noted nineteenth-century poet and publisher, who lived in Roslyn from 1843 until his death in 1878. The original house on the site, on the west bank of Hempstead Harbor, was reputedly built by Richard Kirk, a Quaker farmer, in 1787, passed to William Hicks and was then purchased by Joseph W. Moulton in 1836. Moulton, a historian whose *History of New York State* was published in 1824, modernized the house with a two-story portico in the Greek Revival style. Bryant bought the house from Moulton in 1843 and added a romantic two-story lattice portico that more or less survives today, as well as a kitchen wing. In addition to other interior changes, he constructed a "rustic" library that also survives. Some of these changes were designed by Thomas Wisedall, a New York architect. In 1901 "Cedarmere" was almost completely destroyed by fire, although a part of the first story survived. The

house was reconstructed in accordance with restoration concepts of 1901, an example of which is the late-Federal outer doorway, with fluted Ionic columns, sidelights and transom. The garden plan, however, still reflects Bryant's comprehension of natural beauty (he was one of the principal supporters of Central Park). Bryant was his own landscape architect and the grounds at "Cedarmere" survive today as one of the most romantic vistas to be seen anywhere. Also on the grounds is one of the most architecturally interesting mid-nineteenth-century buildings to survive on Long Island, the Gothic Mill, built around 1860 by Bryant to replace a mill of ca. 1770 on the site that had burned. An elaborately decorated board-and-batten structure set on a high brick foundation, it is embellished with turned pinnacles and prominent drip moldings over the windows. While its architect is unknown, it is possible that Bryant was his own architect. Both the house and the mill were bequeathed to the County of Nassau. (RGG)

72

73

Roslyn Harbor

55

74

75

74. "Clayton," Bryce–Frick Estate (now the Nassau County Museum of Arts)

Northern Boulevard and Mott's Cove Road, Roslyn (open to the public). The Nassau County Museum of Fine Arts occupies the Neo-Georgian Bryce–Frick mansion in Roslyn. Designed ca. 1895 by Ogden Codman, Jr., the great tastemaker and close associate of Edith Wharton, it follows the form and plan he employed for all of his country houses. Codman's client, General Lloyd Bryce, had been Paymaster-General of New York State and founder and editor of the *North American Review*. After Bryce's death in 1917, the estate was purchased by Childs Frick, son of Henry Clay Frick, one of the founders of the U.S. Steel Corporation. The Fricks named the estate "Clayton" and in 1919 retained Sir Charles C. Allom of London to remodel the house to their requirements. Allom, who had established a branch of his firm, White, Allom & Co., in New York, limited his exterior changes to concealment of a few windows and the replacement of the original west entrance porch with a loggia supported by Ionic columns. Sir Charles's interior changes included the installation of the 1740 interior paneling from Stanwick Park, Yorkshire, in the space originally occupied by the drawing room. The grounds at "Clayton" as developed by the Fricks were among the foremost landscapes in America. A more detailed description of that part of the estate may be found in the section on the Milliken–Bevin Trellis [*see* No. 75]. "Clayton," with approximately 150 acres, was acquired by Nassau County in 1969. (RGG)

75. Milliken–Bevin Trellis, Nassau County Museum of Arts

Northern Boulevard, Roslyn (open to the public: 484-9337). Considered one of the most unusual examples of garden architecture in America, the Milliken–Bevin Trellis was designed by the architectural partnership of Henry O. Milliken and Newton P. Bevin in 1931. Located on the grounds of the Lloyd Bryce estate (now the Nassau County Museum of Arts), the trellis was commissioned by Mr. and Mrs. Childs Frick, the subsequent owners, as part of a landscape plan undertaken by noted landscape architect Marian Crugar Coffin. Placed at the south end of a formal parterre, the teak trellis derives from French precedents and consists of an apsidal lattice-lined arch on a raised terrace flanked by clusters of two lattice columns having Ionic capitals and lattice entablatures. Lower collateral trellises extend outward from the two sides of the central arch and curve forward to form a half of a large oval. Originally stained a rich deep green, the trellis deteriorated after Mrs. Frick's death in 1955. However, thanks to a matching grant from the New York State Council on the Arts, the Roslyn Landmark Society has begun restoration of the trellis, the first phase of the structural restoration having been completed in 1989. (RGG)

76. Jerusha Dewey Cottage (now North Hempstead Historical Society)

William Cullen Bryant Nature Preserve, Roslyn Harbor (currently in the process of restoration). In 1865 William Cullen Bryant commissioned a design from the artist and architect Frederick S. Copley for a cottage to be erected on his estate at Roslyn. As originally built, the cottage was a one-and-a-half-story structure with a prominent overhanging pitched roof, richly trimmed with bay windows, multiple eave brackets and pinnacles at each gable peak. The interior of the cottage was simple and it is obvious that both Bryant and Copley regarded it more as a landscape ornament than as an exotic residence. The cottage was rented or loaned in 1866 to Jerusha Dewey, a sister of Dr. Orville Dewey, who was a close friend of Bryant's and one of the foremost theologians of his day. After Bryant's death in 1900, the cottage, together with 180 acres, was sold to Lloyd Bryce, who planned to use it as a guest house. He enlarged the structure by adding a new brick-and-half-timbered lower story beneath the original house. He also added a board-and-batten single-story east wing as well as a two-story wing to the front of the house. In 1969, 165 acres of the estate, including the Dewey Cottage, were sold to the County of Nassau, and in 1981, the cottage was leased to the North Hempstead Historical Society, which is restoring it. (RGG)

77

77. "MONTROSE"

410 Bryant Avenue, Roslyn Harbor (private residence — not open to the public). Built in 1834 by William Hicks, a local sawmill and lumberyard operator, "Montrose" was originally a much smaller, Federal-style house. In 1852 William Cullen Bryant, in residence across the street at "Cedarmere," bought "Montrose" for his daughter Fanny and her husband, Parke Godwin. In 1869 the Godwins retained the noted firm of Vaux, Withers and Company to enlarge their residence. Vaux, in his *Villas and Cottages* of 1857, commented on the alteration of old houses: "without much tearing to pieces, a new quality may be given to a house, if it is only well built at first." This respectful attitude toward original fabric is demonstrated in the Vaux and Withers alteration. Architecturally, the additions were exuberantly Victorian, including a new higher roof capped by a shallow hip with steeply sloping sides and two large facade gables, both pierced by dormer windows of varying shapes and sizes, as well as the addition of stylish paneled chimneys. However, the original shingles, window surrounds and elegant front doorway were left untouched. The interior trim and finish in the Federal part of the house were also preserved. The "Montrose" enlargement conveyed a new sense of style and distinction and produced a house with a significant architectural quality. (RGG)

78. RALLYE MOTORS

Northern Boulevard, Roslyn. The impressive and dramatic building of Rallye Motors, evocative of Art Moderne buildings of the 1930s, is the successful and well-planned design of Ulrich Franzen and Associates. Smooth, unadorned wall surfaces of granite-clad precast concrete and glazed masonry, a low flat roof and curved glass window walls provide a horizontal and streamlined facade, hallmarks of the Art Moderne style. Superbly sited and graded on a six-acre landscaped site, the two-story structure, built in 1988, comprises showroom and customer-service center, connected by a bridge at the second-floor level. The building's architect, Ulrich Franzen, winner of numerous awards including the Gold Medal of the New York Chapter of the AIA, has been engaged in a variety of projects across the country. Among them are a master plan and new facilities for the national enclave at Harper's Ferry, West Virginia, the Alley Theater in Houston, Texas, and new structures for the Hunter College complex in Manhattan. (CT)

78

79

79. ROBESON–WILLIAMS GRIST MILL

Old Northern Boulevard, Roslyn (not open to the public — currently awaiting restoration). A gristmill built on this site by John Robeson as early as 1706 was sold to Jeremiah Williams in 1715. Williams subsequently built a "large and specias [spacious] mill" that survives today. Its construction includes many Dutch framing techniques such as a "bent" system of framing supported by heavy corner braces and notches for the weatherboards on the outer surfaces. This "notching" was a medieval shipbuilding technique used in both England and Holland. However, Jeremiah Williams' mill is the only surviving building in which it has been employed in the Dutch Colonial area of the United States. Although, as part of a restoration project carried out in 1916, the exterior was clad in concrete molded to look like the original weatherboards, much of the mill's highly unusual Dutch-type framing has survived, as well as the late eighteenth-century milling equipment and the original seventeenth-century millpond. Acquired by the Nassau County Museum in the mid-1970s, it awaits restoration. (RGG) *79: The Gristmill, 1987. 79A: Interior, showing post-and-beam construction.*

79A

80

80. ROSLYN HIGHLANDS FIREHOUSE

Warner Avenue, Roslyn (can be seen from the road). The Roslyn Highlands Company's award-winning 1985 firehouse at Roslyn Heights is proof that good design can be achieved even on a limited budget. Designed by the Spector Group, the North Hills firm responsible for such major new Long Island buildings as the EAB Plaza and Grumman Data Systems, the 12,500-square-foot fire-protection facility received the Award for Design Excellence from the Masonry Institute. Although the building is contemporary in appearance, the architects sought a design solution that would combine "the firehouse's historical role with its functional purpose." Hence, a sense of historical context was achieved for this Postmodern structure through the inclusion of such features as a bell tower, balconies, string courses and "traditional fire-engine-red detailing." (RBM)

81. TRINITY EPISCOPAL CHURCH

Northern Boulevard and Church Street, Roslyn (open to the public). Designed by the noted architect Stanford White, of McKim, Mead & White, and donated by wealthy socialite Mrs. Clarence Mackay, Trinity Episcopal was built in 1906 to replace an earlier board-and-batten church. Although White designed few churches, he was the architect for the Judson Memorial on Washington Square in New York City and two country churches, of which Trinity is the more ambitious. The building, constructed of stacked courses of clinker-brick headers, is derived in part from the transitional Norman–Early English Revival style. The round-arched windows and bell-cote are part of a combination of design elements used romantically. Cruciform in plan, the interior of the church is dominated by the superb framing of the high roof vault, which employs soaring wooden trusses in the English late-medieval tradition, resting on hammerbeams and supported by massive wooden knees. McKim, Mead & White's drawings for the roof framing survive and specify the use of yellow pine for the trusses, hammerbeams and associated timbers. The two west transept windows were made by Tiffany Studios and bear its label. Although much altered, the original Parish House was also designed by White. (RGG)

81

82. OBADIAH WASHINGTON VALENTINE HOUSE AND GAZEBO

105 Main Street, Roslyn (private residence — not open to the public). Roslyn was little influenced by the Greek Revival style, the Valentine house being one of only two "temple-fronted" houses in the village. Its most visible, strongly Greek Revival exterior feature is the elegant sidelighted and transomed principal doorway, derived from Plate 28 of Asher Benjamin's *Practical House Carpenter* (Boston, 1830). There is also a two-story east porch fitted with octagonal columns in the Greek Revival manner. The house almost certainly was erected by Thomas Wood, who built most of the Main Street houses. In 1911 east and west "shed" dormer windows and a single-story gabled north wing were added, to which the present owners added a story in 1985. Apart from these alterations, the house has survived almost without change and incorporates several interesting outbuildings. One of these, a gazebo of ca. 1860 moved from Cutchogue, is a lattice-walled, octagonal structure, four of whose walls are pierced with concave-arched doorways in the "Moorish" style. The principal feature of the building is its octagonal concave roof, constructed of a solid layer of beaded boards capped by a vigorous turned pinnacle. Another outbuilding, a Gothic summerhouse (originally with a privy behind it), was relocated from "Clifton" in Roslyn Harbor. (RGG) *82A: The gazebo.*

83. WILLIAM M. VALENTINE HOUSE (NOW ROSLYN VILLAGE HALL)

1 Paper Mill Road, Roslyn (open to the public). Originally a Federal-style shingled, two-and-a-half story, three-bay-wide hall house having a two-story kitchen wing, the William M. Valentine house was built about 1800 east of an earlier paper mill on the site. In 1775 Hendrick Onderdonk, John Remsen and Hugh Gaine dammed a pond in Roslyn and built the first paper mill in New York State, mainly to guarantee a source of paper for Gaine's *New York Mercury*. In 1801 the paper mill and surrounding lands were bought by Valentine. He, and later his descendants, operated the mill until it closed a century later. During the Civil War, William M. Valentine, second son of William, expanded the house to a five-bay-wide center-hall plan and added a mansard roof capped by a belvedere. The Federal and Civil War–period interiors have survived almost unaltered. The house, in Valentine family ownership until 1911, was acquired by the Bryant Library Association in 1952. Restored by the Incorporated Village of Roslyn in 1963 and relocated to the south side of Paper Mill Road, it continues to serve Roslyn today as the Village Hall. (RGG)

84. VAN NOSTRAND–STARKINS HOUSE

221 Main Street, Roslyn (open to the public). The Van Nostrand–Starkins house, built ca. 1680, is probably the earliest surviving house in Nassau County. The original 20' × 16' house was built in the medieval English tradition with a steeply pitched roof and was framed in American white oak, almost all of which has survived, including major segments of the original sills. During the second quarter of the eighteenth century the house was enlarged, possibly by the joiner who framed the Robeson–Williams Gristmill [*see* No. 79], with a 9-foot-wide lean-to addition along the north wall. During this period the west wall and part of the east were sheathed with chamfered-butt shingles, some of which have survived. Extensions were added to the south rafters to create a projecting overhang with a concave profile in the Dutch manner. A one-and-a-half-story east wing was constructed ca. 1880 with little impact on the original building, and the house was painted a reddish-brown color. The Van Nostrand–Starkins house was restored by the Roslyn Landmark Society in the 1970s in accordance with a plan completed by John R. Stevens and is open to the public on Saturday afternoons from May through October. (RGG)

85. ELLEN E. WARD MEMORIAL CLOCK TOWER

Old Northern Boulevard and Main Street, Roslyn. Donated and built in memory of Ellen E. Ward (1826–1893), who was deeply interested in the Roslyn community and much involved in local charities, the Memorial Clock Tower was erected in 1895. It stands in a small landscaped triangle formed by Old Northern Boulevard, Main Street and Tower Street. The architects were Lamb & Rich of New York, who were also the architects of Theodore Roosevelt's "Sagamore Hill" in Oyster Bay. The clock tower is a four-story building that tapers slightly to a pyramidal, Spanish-tiled roof. The obelisklike shape of the principal tower probably is the reason for its description as "Egyptian," although stylistically it would be called "Richardsonian" today. Four rusticated piers rise above the third story with its prominent eaves. The original clock mechanism by the Seth Thomas Clock Company survives and is fully functional. (RGG)

84

85

86

87

86. WARREN S. WILKEY HOUSE

190 Main Street, Roslyn (private residence — not open to the public). Warren S. Wilkey, a native of Roslyn who became a lawyer and merchant in New York City, built this five-bay-wide house in 1864 in the Second Empire Style. Commodious by local standards, it is sheathed with novelty siding, which appeared in the United States as early as 1850. Capped by a slightly concave slate mansard roof that rests upon an elaborately scrolled bracketed cornice, the entire roof-cornice complex — the principal architectural feature of the house — is derived from the Hart M. Schiff house built in New York by the well-known architect Detlef Lienau. The simple but impressive interior includes the earliest known bathroom in Roslyn having inside plumbing. The Wilkey house included a number of ingenious solutions to domestic problems such as the early use of a "pass-through" window from the kitchen to the pantry and "counter-plaster" insulation in the walls that was so effective it was retained as part of the modern insulation plan. The house was restored during the 1970s by the Roslyn Preservation Corporation, the local, not-for-profit revolving restoration fund, and stands today as a superb example of how the finest-quality restoration of a derelict building can stimulate the upgrading of an entire neighborhood. (RGG)

87. "HEMPSTEAD HOUSE" (NOW SANDS POINT PARK AND PRESERVE)

Middleneck Road, Sands Point (open to the public: 883-1610). "Hempstead House," built for Howard Gould between 1910 and 1912, was designed by the prominent architectural firm of Hunt & Hunt. Richard Howland Hunt (1862–1931), son of the famous architect Richard Morris Hunt, the first American to study architecture at the École des Beaux-Arts in Paris, had formed a partnership with his brother Joseph in 1901; their most important commissions included the east wing of the Metropolitan Museum and the 69th Street Armory. Built of rough stone with limestone trim, "Hempstead House" is based on English manor houses of the Tudor period. Tudor details include the use of the flattened arch for the entrance portico and the graceful trefoil lancet windows grouped within simple stone hood molds. The varied roofline, another Tudor characteristic, is dominated by a square and a circular tower, both crowned with mock fortifications. Inside, a formal Beaux-Arts–inspired plan prevailed, with a skylighted palm court and a glass-enclosed terrace on an axis with the large living room — all three forming a tremendous Great Hall. In 1917 Daniel Guggenheim, philanthropist and promoter of aviation, purchased the property, which included the main house and stable complex [see No. 88], and it was here at "Hempstead House" that the first significant financing of United States aviation and rocketry was implemented. In 1946 the U.S. Navy purchased the house and stable for its Naval Training Devices Center. In 1971 the property was given to the Nassau County Museum for use as a park–preserve and is open to the public from May to October. (CT)

88. "CASTLE GOULD" (NOW SANDS POINT PARK AND PRESERVE)

Middleneck Road, Sands Point (open to the public: 883-1610). "Castle Gould," part of the original complex planned by railroad heir Howard Gould, son of Wall Street financier Jay Gould, was one of 14 structures on this Sands Point country estate [see No. 87]. Ireland's Kilkenny Castle in particular and the Medieval Revival in general influenced the design of the massive turreted building, formerly the equestrian-parade stables and now the site of the visitor reception center and the Americana storage–study collection, which is available for study and browsing in one wing of "Castle Gould." Designed in 1902 by Augustus N. Allen (1868–1958), the castellated structure, with its robust stonework and drum-shaped towers, incorporated a U-shaped stable on one side and a rectangular carriage area on the other. One of the largest estate service buildings on Long Island, the complex housed servants' quarters on the second floor. The stables, along with the main house, were sold to Daniel Guggenheim in 1917 and in 1971 both were deeded to Nassau County. The main house, "Hempstead House," and "Castle Gould" are open to the public May through October. (CT)

88

89

89. "The Woodshed"

115 Central Avenue, Sea Cliff (private residence — not open to the public). "The Woodshed," Long Island's candidate for the nation's most exuberant Stick Style building, was built as a summer boardinghouse by John Wood, the operator of a Manhattan gymnasium. Now a private residence, the polychromatic building exhibits the hallmarks of its style, which reached the zenith of its popularity in the 1870s. The tall proportions, large brackets, sharp roof angles and diagonal "stick work" on the facade are all characteristics of this truth-in-architecture movement, in which exterior elements reflected the unseen frame within the walls. Restored by the present owners, "The Woodshed" has been given a new lease on life as a handsome reminder of Sea Cliff's resort history. (RBM)

90

90. "WOODSIDE," JAMES A. BURDEN ESTATE (NOW WOODCREST COUNTRY CLUB)

Muttontown Road, Syosset (private club — not open to the public). In the world of country house building, architects cultivated clients by living among them. For William Adams Delano (of Delano & Aldrich), the opportunity came in 1909 when an attorney building in Muttontown lent him the capital to create an estate of his own. Thus began a 20-year surge in the construction of elegant houses and gardens designed for a style of country life quite unlike that of Newport and other summering places à la mode. Iron manufacturer James A. Burden's "Woodside," built in 1917, not far from Delano's own "Muttontown Corners," is a stately Adamesque villa with quiet presence in its broad pediment and widely spaced openings. Notwithstanding formal gardens, grassy terraces and tennis courts, "Woodside" was a house of straightforward warmth, true to the hand of its designer and has, since 1960, functioned as the clubhouse for the Woodcrest Country Club. (EF) *90: The house, in an old view. 90A: The club, 1991.*

90A

91

92

91. EAB Plaza

Hempstead Turnpike, Uniondale (open to the public). Reaching a height of 15 stories above the Hempstead Plain, the twin towers of the huge 1.1 million-square-foot EAB Plaza at Uniondale can be seen from miles away, heralding the presence of one of the largest suburban office centers in the tristate region. Designed by the Spector Group, the 1984 complex, characterized by its elliptical facades and reflecting glass, boasts a spectacular example of a feature introduced by Beaux-Arts architects at the turn of the century: the palm court or winter garden. The EAB Plaza's version, described by the architects as a "tropical atrium of waterfalls and foliage lying beneath a great glass dome," and the nearby fountain (which doubles as a skating rink in winter) are notable public amenities. (RBM)

92. Central High School

Fletcher Avenue, Valley Stream (public school — can be seen from the road). Valley Stream's Modernistic Central High School, completed in 1929 to the designs of Frederic P. Wiedersum, is included here as a reminder of the legacy of handsome pre–World War II school architecture on Long Island. Wiedersum was the architect of many of those buildings between 1929 and 1954; he received commissions for 215 schools in the tristate area, the greatest concentration being in Nassau County. (RBM)

SUFFOLK

HIGHWAY FIRSTS

A

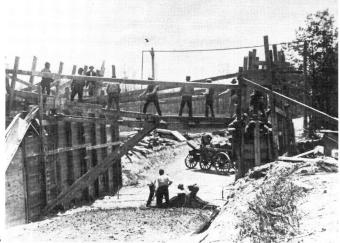

B

C

*L*ong Island has long been the scene of highway innovations. The opening of the Erie Canal and the arrival of "cheap" Western grain led to the construction of one of the nation's greatest concentrations of privately financed turnpikes and plank roads in the nineteenth century as local farmers were forced to concentrate on perishable crops that had to be rushed to market. The arrival of the combustion engine and the region's development as a resort led to the creation of William K. Vanderbilt, Jr.'s 48-mile Long Island Motor Parkway (incorporated in 1906), the first limited-access, grade- and crossing-free vehicular toll road in America. Its gate lodges and terminal inn, the Petit Trianon, designed by John Russell Pope, at Lake Ronkonkoma (burned 1957), were also to be influential precursors of later highway facilities. While primarily used for family outings and to test one's "motor" (the parkway's stockholders were automobile owners and manufacturers), it also foresaw the concept of using the automobile to improve one's lifestyle. The Parkway's chief engineer, A. R. Pardington, writing in *Harper's Weekly* in 1907, noted that, once the Queensboro (59th Street) Bridge had been completed, a businessman seeking a little recreation could leave his Manhattan office in the late afternoon, arrive at the western entrance of the Parkway in 20 minutes and reach Riverhead or Southampton before the electric lights began to "twinkle."

Accessing public parks and recreation by specially designed highways, however, was to await public financing and a man who did not drive a car, Robert Moses. The great builder was to be responsible for 200 miles of parkways on Long Island. The Grand Central, Belt, Laurelton,

D

Cross Island, Interborough, Wantagh, Sagtikos, Mead-owbrook, Sunken Meadow, Northern and Southern State were all his creations, not to mention the parks to which they connected and the Long Island Expressway. Based on landscape concepts introduced by Frederick Law Olmsted and Calvert Vaux in the development of Central Park (1858–ca. 1880), and taken a step further in the seminal Bronx River Parkway (1916–24, the first public toll- and crossing-free, limited-access parkway built within a ribbon of parkland), Moses' picturesque roads, with their rustic bridges and appointments, popularized the parkway in America. He is credited with introducing everything from the Sunday drive to systematic vehicular travel, and his Meadowbrook Causeway to Jones Beach, which opened in October 1934, was the first fully divided limited-access highway in the nation. Completed seven months before the first German autobahn, Meadowbrook was hailed as a model of articulation between highway and residential development. Moses' lavishly landscaped and curvilinear parkways were also innovative for their 400-foot rights-of-way, absence of billboards and carbon black–tinted pavement designed to contrast with the white curbs and acceleration lanes. (RBM)

A: Races on the Motor Parkway near Hauppauge, ca. 1910. B: Workers lay sections of the Long Island Motor Parkway, 1907. C: Motor Parkway Inn (Petit Trianon), designed by John Russell Pope, ca. 1911. D: Aerial view of the Meadowbrook Parkway. E: Police barracks, Southern State Parkway, 1928. F: Northern State Parkway, 1930s.

E

F

93. MISS AMELIA'S COTTAGE

Montauk Highway and Windmill Lane, Amagansett (open to the public: 267-3020). Named for Amelia Schellinger (1841–1930), who lived in the house much of her life, the cottage is a compact structure of one story with a center door and chimney characteristic of its early form. The Schellingers, who came to Amagansett from Staten Island in the 1660s, were successful in offshore whaling and commercial shipping, and were prominent in the community in the eighteenth and nineteenth centuries. Several houses of a later era were built by Schellingers and remain standing along Amagansett's main thoroughfare. The house has been preserved since 1963 by the Amagansett Historical Association.

Believed to have been built ca. 1725, the structure is of vertical plank construction that is associated with other early eighteenth-century period work in the area. The interior plan preserves two principal rooms flanking the center chimney, a kitchen at the back with smaller rooms at either side, and a staircase to the garret that rises in two directions from a center landing. Architectural details of the eighteenth and nineteenth centuries, such as a Federal-period cupboard and mantelpiece, are intact, providing a setting for the society's collection of local artifacts. The museum is open to the public June through Labor Day. (ZS)

94. ROBERT GWATHMEY HOUSE AND STUDIO

Bluff Road, Amagansett (private residence — not open to the public). The 1965 Gwathmey house is a masterpiece of the "Neo-Corb" generation of 1960s architecture and a prime example of the house as object-in-space. The main house and smaller guest house/ studio, designed by the young Charles Gwathmey just three years out of Yale's School of Architecture and in his first partnership as Gwathmey & Henderson, became prototypes for vacation homes all over the East Coast, inspiring countless imitations. Few, if any, have been as effective as the original. The two buildings command the space that surrounds them. Deftly modeled arrangements of geometric volumes, sheathed in vertical cedar siding, they are planted like two Cubist sculptures, mother and child, on a flat green table. (AG)

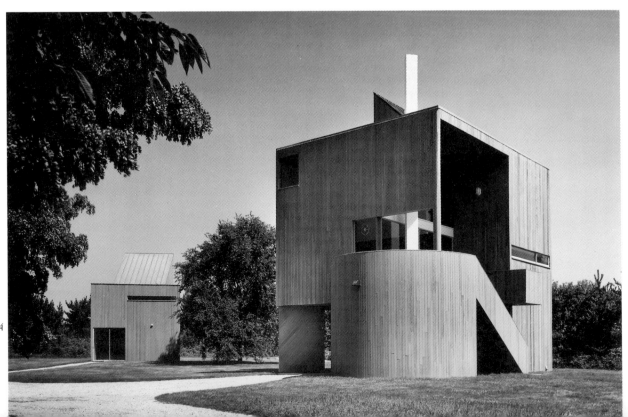

95

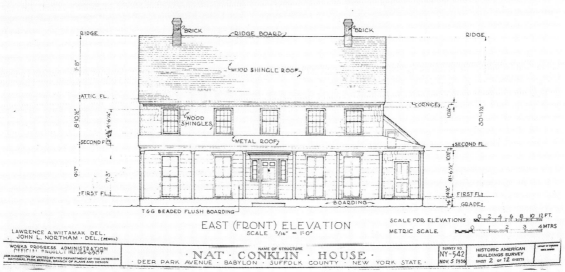

RIDGE   BRICK   RIDGE BOARD   BRICK   RIDGE

WOOD SHINGLE ROOF

ATTIC FL.

WOOD SHINGLES

CORNICE

SECOND FL.   METAL ROOF   SECOND FL.

FIRST FL.   FIRST FL.

GRADE

T & G BEADED FLUSH BOARDING   BOARDING

EAST (FRONT) ELEVATION
SCALE 3/16" = 1'-0"

SCALE FOR ELEVATIONS   0 2 4 6 8 10 12 FT.
METRIC SCALE   0 1 2 3 4 MTRS

LAWRENCE A. WHITAMAK DEL.
JOHN L. NORTHAM DEL. (PENCIL)

WORKS PROGRESS ADMINISTRATION
OFFICIAL PROJECT NO. 265-6907
DER DIRECTION OF UNITED STATES DEPARTMENT OF THE INTERIOR
NATIONAL PARK SERVICE, BRANCH OF PLANS AND DESIGN

NAME OF STRUCTURE
· NAT · CONKLIN · HOUSE ·
· DEER PARK AVENUE · BABYLON · SUFFOLK COUNTY · NEW YORK STATE ·

SURVEY NO.
NY-542
NOV. 5 1936

HISTORIC AMERICAN
BUILDINGS SURVEY
SHEET 2 OF 12 SHEETS

95A

95. NATHANIEL CONKLIN HOUSE

Deer Park Avenue, Babylon (open to the public). The Nathaniel Conklin house, built in 1803 at the intersection of Deer Park Avenue and Main Street in Babylon, was moved a few blocks north to the Washington Hotel complex in 1871. Conklin, a successful local businessman and landowner, is credited with naming the village and inscribing "New Babylon" on a chimney tablet. This large, two-story, center-hall house served as both residence and store in the mid-nineteenth century until its site was acquired for commercial development by David S. S. Sammis, an entrepreneur and hotel-builder. In an era of rapid expansion for the village, the Conklin house was relocated to John Lux's Washington Hotel grounds near the railroad tracks, where it served first as a residence, then a boardinghouse at the turn of the century. Vacant by the late 1930s, it was measured and drawn by the Historic American Buildings Survey, which recognized its landmark status. Through the generosity of Sammis descendants, the structure was later given to the American Red Cross and served as a headquarters for the local Babylon Unit from 1945 to 1988. Despite a history of changing use and neglect, the Nathaniel Conklin house preserves much of its early detailing such as Federal-period mantelpieces and doors, window sashes of the 8-over-8 and 12-over-12 type, and a central staircase with delicately turned newel posts. It will soon serve the Village of Babylon as a historic house museum and cultural center coadministered by the Babylon Historical and Preservation Society. (ZS) *95A: East elevation.*

96

97

Bay Shore

74

96. SINAI REFORM TEMPLE [DESTROYED BY FIRE]

39 Brentwood Road, Bay Shore. This unusual Neo-Expressionist synagogue, a 1964 design of Harold Edelman and Stanley Salzman, is noteworthy for the Star of David floor plan of its sanctuary, which was chosen as both a symbolic statement and a means of bringing seating closer to the ark. An adjacent and connected social hall that is just a level removed from the sanctuary allows for expansion of seating and ease of circulation. The temple's roof doubles as the exterior wall. The frame, comprised of laminated 2″ × 6″ beams sheathed with ¾″ plywood, was fabricated at the site. (RBM)

97. ST. PATRICK'S R.C. CHURCH

Main Street, Bay Shore (accessible to the public). Designed by the New York architect Gustave E. Steinbeck, this ambitious basilica was built in 1919, when the South Shore community was a popular resort town. The handsome Romanesque building, enlivened by its corbeled cornices, diaper-pattern brickwork and massive buttresses, replaced a modest wooden chapel. The brick-lined interior is characterized by its open timber ceilings, terracotta ornamentation and frescoes on the dome and walls of the sanctuary executed by the Rambusch Decorating Company. (RBM) [*For Bay Shore see also No. 107.*]

98. PRICE HOUSE

255 Gillette Avenue, Bayport (private residence — not open to the public). A little corner of Los Angeles transported to Long Island, this well-preserved house designed by Richard Neutra (1892–1970) sits at the center of a manicured lawn that sweeps down to a bulkhead at the water's edge. It is very much the Modernist vision of an object in space, and very well united to its waterfront setting. Interior living spaces slip effortlessly out onto the surrounding lawn. Its large expanses of glass, fieldstone chimney and walls, and redwood "outrigger" beams and posts were all trademarks of this modern master's post–World War II oeuvre. It is apparently the only extant house by Neutra on the East Coast, the Brown house on Fisher's Island, one of Neutra's most important residential commissions, built in 1938, having burned to the ground in 1975. (AG)

99

100

99. OSBORN–MOTT HOUSE (NOW GATEWAY THEATRE)

South Country Road, Bellport (accessible to the public).
Built about 1827 for Charles Osborn of New York, this shingled, gambrel-roofed house of imposing proportions is remarkable for its entrance with elaborate leaded sidelights and transom. Paired end chimneys, of which two remain, a projecting cornice with modillions and pedimented dormers emphasize the high roof. In 1884, J. L. B. Mott, a wealthy New Yorker, bought the property as a summer home and in 1890 commissioned Stanford White of McKim, Mead & White to design the west wing, which was destroyed by fire in 1962. Photographs show a large-scale gambrel-roof addition that contained a Tudor style ballroom. The Motts owned the property until the 1940s, when the house and several outbuildings became the home of the Gateway Theatre, considered to be among the top summer-stock theaters in America. (EW)

100. BELLPORT METHODIST CHURCH

185 South Country Road, Bellport (accessible to the public).
Built in 1850, this handsome example of a Greek Revival vernacular church projects the mid-nineteenth-century concept of "muscular Christianity," appropriately expressed here in a large-scale Doric order. Raised on a plinthlike brick basement, the temple front displays a pedimented gable with full entablature, both decorated with large dentils and turned moldings resting on four Doric pilasters. A two-stage bell tower, also decorated with cornices and Doric pilasters, supports an octagonal spire with a graceful finial ball marking the top. Originally erected as a Presbyterian church on land donated by the Charles Osborn family [*see* No. 99], the building was acquired by the Methodist community in 1945 and today it continues to serve as their house of worship. (EW)

101. BRENTWOOD SCHOOLHOUSE

Third Avenue, Brentwood (currently awaiting restoration). Built in 1857 by the residents of Modern Times, a utopian community that flourished in what is now Brentwood from 1851 to 1864, the octagonal building is one of eight surviving structures on Long Island inspired by the writings of Orson Squire Fowler and the only example of an octagonal schoolhouse. Fowler, a nineteenth-century phrenologist, contended that eight-sided buildings were more practical since corners wasted space [see No. 176]. After the collapse of the freethinking Modern Times, which had attracted national attention and controversy, the unusual schoolhouse continued to serve Brentwood until it was replaced by a new facility in 1907 and converted to a residence. In 1989 this National Register landmark was moved by the Town of Islip to the Anthony F. Felicio Administration Center at Third Avenue, Brentwood, where the Brentwood Historical Society plans to raise funds to restore it. (RBM)

102. BEEBE WINDMILL

Ocean Road, Bridgehampton (museum — open to the public: 283-6000). The Beebe Windmill, erected in Sag Harbor in 1820, was the last windmill built on eastern Long Island. Because of its late date of construction it contains innovations in windmill technology that had just arrived in America from England. Dramatic new devices were developed by English millwrights utilizing newly available accurate iron castings. The Beebe Windmill, built by Samuel Schellinger, was outfitted with some of this new machinery, including a fantail to rotate the cap automatically to face the sails into the wind, cast-iron bevel gearing, and centrifugal governors to adjust the millstones automatically to grind a consistently fine flour. The machinery introduced in the Beebe Windmill was later installed in most other Long Island windmills. In 1837, the Beebe Windmill was moved to Bridgehampton, where it operated until 1911. The mill is now owned by the Town of Southampton and open as a museum. (RH)

LONG ISLAND WINDMILLS

A

B

*T*he largest regional grouping of early American windmills is found on eastern Long Island. Here 11 windmills, built from 1795 to 1820 for the purpose of grinding grain, document the evolution of a particular technology in America.

The flat landscape of eastern Long Island provides few sites suitable for watermills. From the beginning, the settlers relied on the power of the wind to grind grain, saw wood and accomplish other tasks. The earliest recorded windmill here was constructed in Southold in 1644, four years after the town was settled. The windmills of this early period were of a type called post mills. All the machinery was contained in a small house that sat on top of a massive post. The house was turned on top of this post by a large lever, called a tail pole, so that the sails could be kept faced into the wind as the wind shifted direction. The post mills constructed here were based on English examples and the evolution of windmills on eastern Long Island from 1644 to 1820 closely followed the development of the English windmill. No early post mills survive in this country today.

All the 11 extant Long Island windmills are smock mills, which were first constructed here in the late eighteenth century. The smock mill is distinguished from the post mill by having a stationary octagonal tower housing the millstones, surmounted by a cap holding the sails. The cap can be revolved on the tower to keep the sails facing into the wind. The earliest smock mill surviving on Long Island was built on Gardiners Island in 1795. The simple, direct gearing to power one pair of millstones and the tail pole of the post mill were carried over to this early smock mill. In the early nineteenth century more sophisticated wooden gearing drove multiple pairs of millstones and was used to revolve the cap as well. The Hook Windmill, built in East Hampton in 1806, displays the most advanced stage of wooden gearing. The Beebe Windmill of 1820 introduced cast-iron gearing and other innovations developed in England and made possible by the production of accurate iron castings. These innovations included the fantail, which would automatically revolve the cap. The Beebe Windmill, the last built on Long Island, marks the transition from the age of wooden technology into the era of iron machinery.

Although steam-powered gristmills appeared on eastern Long Island by 1850, the windmills continued to operate throughout the nineteenth century, serving the relatively isolated farming villages. Today, four of these windmills are open to the public as museums: Windmill at Water Mill; Pantigo and Hook Windmills in East Hampton; and the Beebe Windmill in Southampton. (RH)

A: East Marion Windmill (no longer extant), ca. 1870.
B: Isometric drawing of Beebe Windmill (1820), Bridgehampton. C: Gardiners Island Windmill.
D: Wooden wheel, Gardiners Island wind-powered sawmill. E: Long Island's existing windmills.

C

D

E

1. Mill Hill Windmill
2. Good Ground Windmill
3. Windmill at Water Mill
4. Beebe Windmill
5. Wainscott Windmill
6. Hook Windmill
7. Pantigo Windmill
8. Gardiner Windmill
9. Hayground Windmill
10. Gardiners Island Windmill
11. Shelter Island Windmill

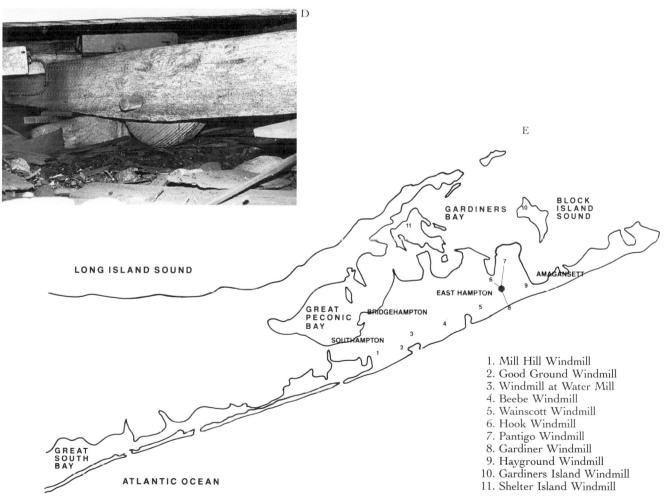

LONG ISLAND SOUND

GARDINERS BAY

BLOCK ISLAND SOUND

AMAGANSETT

EAST HAMPTON

GREAT PECONIC BAY

BRIDGEHAMPTON

SOUTHAMPTON

GREAT SOUTH BAY

ATLANTIC OCEAN

103.

103. "HAMPTON HOUSE"

Main Street and Ocean Road, Bridgehampton (private residence — not open to the public). "Hampton House" was built ca. 1840 by Nathan Rogers, a painter of miniatures, and the building acquired its name in 1885 when it was converted for use as a hotel during the decline of the once-prosperous whaling industry. Its five-bay, two-story center block preserves a full-facade porch supported on four Ionic columns, a form more commonly associated with the Greek Revival style of the Southeastern states. The impressive columns are echoed by pilasters at the corners of the block and two flanking wings; a roofline balustrade that at one time graced the main house was destroyed by the hurricane of 1938. Also lacking its decorative rooftop cupola as a result of that catastrophe, the house retains other features that are characteristic of the Greek Revival idiom, such as its front-door surround made up of pilasters topped with a frieze and cornice with Ionic columns framing the inset entryway. (KB)

104. MECOX FIELDS HOUSES

Bridgehampton (private residences — not open to the public). Surely one of the most prolific (and imitated) architects working on the eastern end of Long Island in the 1970s and 1980s, Robert A. M. Stern set the tone for the neotraditional look in residential architecture that was the preferred style of the 1980s. In his designs for such individual houses as the Bozzi house in East Hampton, Stern has borrowed liberally from the Shingle Style traditions of Long Island's resort architecture. He has also designed some of the most successful residential developments in the area, including Mecox Fields (1983–85), a group of houses set around a serpentine road in the style of a nineteenth-century suburban subdivision. While each house is different, they are all united by a similar use of cedar shingles stained gray, white trim, large chimneys, trellis work, circular and half-circle windows, sweeping gable roofs and dormer windows. (AG)

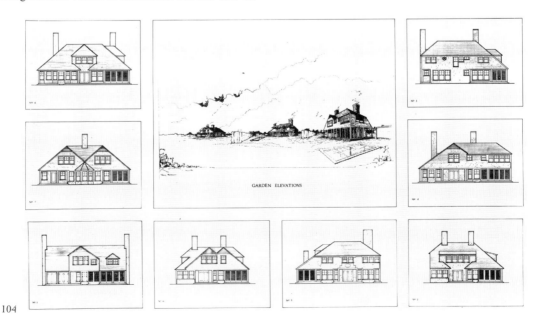

104.

GARDEN ELEVATIONS

105. FRANCES BREESE MILLER HOUSE

Bridgehampton (private residence — not open to the public).
An important early example of "beach-house modern," this small
house was originally built in 1933 for $7500 by its owner, Frances
Breese Miller, an artist and designer who had been inspired by the
modern architecture she had seen at an exposition in Stockholm.
She hired Long Island–based architect Lansing "Denny" Holden
to draw up plans to her specifications. "I wanted floor-to-ceiling
windows and exposure to the sun on all sides," wrote Miller in her
memoirs. "Even the bathroom must have sun, and most important,
a view from the bathtub," she wrote. "Tradition would be abandoned. No covered porches, no attics, no dining room, no maids
. . . ." No matter where you stand in the "Sandbox," as the house is
named, you become aware of the surrounding windswept scenery
with views to the south of the Atlantic Ocean and to the north of
the calmer waters of Mecox Bay. Nature seems to intrude everywhere, pressing in through each window and door, the crest of one
giant dune practically breaking through a large plate-glass window into the living room. (AG)

105

106. SAM'S CREEK DEVELOPMENT

**Sam's Creek Road, Bridgehampton (private residences — not
open to the public).** Sam's Creek Development, designed by the
Bridgehampton architect Norman Jaffe, winner of numerous
Archi awards, is one of the more original and well-conceived
house groupings on eastern Long Island. The four structures fit
comfortably into their potato-field setting and prove the point that
a flat-roofed, Modernist building vocabulary can be as effectively
"contextual" (especially in low-lying beach areas) as pitched roofs
and cedar-shingle siding. The designs won an Archi Award in
1980. (AG) *106A: A panorama of the development.*

106

106A

107

107. SAGTIKOS MANOR

Montauk Highway, West Bay Shore (open to the public). Albert B. Corey, the late New York State historian, called it "one of the most distinguished historic houses in the United States" and since then the manor house and ten surrounding acres have been placed on the National Register of Historic Places and the property has been declared a Historic District by the Town of Islip. The manor house includes three architecturally distinct sections. The oldest section was built between 1692 and 1697 by Stephanus Van Cortlandt, who also built Van Cortlandt Manor on the Hudson River. The middle section was built ca. 1772 by Isaac Thompson, whose father bought the 1200-acre farm in the mid-1750s and afterwards gifted it to son Isaac upon his marriage to Mary Gardiner of the Gardiners Island family. The final and largest additions were built by Frederick Diodati Thompson in 1905 under the supervision of the Riverhead-born architect Isaac H.

Green. They include a high-ceilinged drawing room on the east end, an elegant dining room on the west end and a three-story gambrel-roofed section with kitchen and service rooms on the ground floor, family and servants' bedrooms above. The second-floor bedrooms of the older sections include those occupied by General Sir Henry Clinton during the American Revolution, and by President George Washington during his 1790 tour of Long Island. The property, in Thompson–Gardiner ownership since the mid-1700s, is owned and maintained by Robert D. L. Gardiner, who recently announced that he has transferred it to a trust to assure its upkeep and preservation. Many of the rooms, a large brick-walled garden and the family cemetery are on view to visitors during the summer months, with docents of the Sagtikos Manor Historical Society acting as guides. (CS) [*For Bay Shore see also Nos. 96 & 97.*]

108. OLD SOUTH HAVEN PRESBYTERIAN CHURCH

368 South Country Road (corner Beaver Dam Road), Brookhaven (open to the public on a limited basis). In 1740 the Presbyterian congregation established a church in South Haven that was desecrated during the Revolution. The present church, built on the same site in 1828, was saved from destruction in 1961 and moved to the hamlet of Brookhaven. A shingled Federal style church of gentle proportions, it has a projecting belltower entrance with arched door and window. Flanking the tower on the

front are two windows at the second-story level, and three large arched windows articulate each side of the nave. The pedimented gable, the eaves and cornice returns are decorated with modillions, as is the two-stage tower that supports an octagonal spire with ball finial. The period weather vane is a replica in gilded wood of a trout caught in Carman's River by Daniel Webster, on the occasion of attending services in South Haven, an event commemorated in a Currier & Ives print. (EW)

109. CEDAR ISLAND LIGHTHOUSE

Cedar Point, East Hampton (accessible to the public). As if it were an arctic bird blown off course by a winter gale, the Cedar Island Lighthouse appears out of place on Eastern Long Island. The handsome two-and-a-half story, L-shaped structure would have been more at home along the Boston waterfront or Maine's rugged coast, for it is an example of the Boston Granite school of the middle decades of the nineteenth century. A wooden building

was first erected in 1839. The present structure arose in 1868 and exhibits the trabeated construction techniques and rough-cut ashlar walls that make this style so interesting and appropriate for lighthouses. An important navigational aid for Sag Harbor–bound mariners until it was discontinued in 1934, the lighthouse was built by the W. & J. Beattie Company of Fall River, Massachusetts. (RBM)

108

109

110. PRESBYTERIAN CHURCH OF THE MORICHES

464 Main Street, Center Moriches (open to the public: 878-1993). Founded in 1748 and incorporated in 1839, the Presbyterian Church of the Moriches now preserves its original Greek Revival–period sanctuary within a much-enlarged edifice dating from 1886. The later church building incorporates intricate exterior detailing associated with the Stick Style, including a variety of wood-shingle patterns, applied diagonal boarding and projecting dormers and stoops that contribute to its lively and asymmetrical composition. The steeple dominates the design and rises at the southeast corner of the structure where two main entrances are located. An open belfry at the third story level preserves the "J. H. Thompson N-York" bell from the original 1839 church, and supports a tapering spire once crowned by a decorative weather vane. Restoration of the ornamental steeple shingles was undertaken in 1982 with help from the Town of Brookhaven Community Development Agency. (ZS)

111. SUYDAM HOUSE (GREENLAWN–CENTERPORT HISTORICAL ASSOCIATION)

Route 25A and Centerport Road, Centerport (undergoing restoration). Now perched precariously close to Route 25A and Centerport Road, the Suydam House is the earliest surviving structure in this waterfront hamlet, located just east of Huntington. Although its origins are as yet undocumented, the house has been associated with the Suydam family since the late eighteenth century. It has been continuously occupied and will become the home of the Greenlawn–Centerport Historical Association, which plans to administer the farmhouse as a museum facility. Structural evidence suggests that the house evolved through at least four stages, beginning with a small 14′ × 13′ cell dating from the early eighteenth century. Additions to the back, east and, finally, west sides apparently took place as successive generations enlarged the dwelling for their own purposes. Restoration of the house will highlight the architectural evolution of this typical one-and-a-half-story Long Island farmhouse. (ZS)

112. "EAGLE'S NEST" (NOW VANDERBILT MUSEUM)

180 Little Neck Road, Centerport (museum—open to the public: 261-5656). The palatial Spanish Baroque country estate of William K. Vanderbilt II (1878–1944) in Centerport, "Eagle's Nest," evolved over more than two decades as a personal evocation of Mediterranean and Spanish motifs garnered from many trips east. Around 1910, Whitney Warren, a cousin of Vanderbilt's and a partner in the prominent architectural firm of Warren & Wetmore (architects, along with Reed & Stem, of Grand Central Terminal, completed in 1913), was chosen to design a modest bachelor's retreat that included a small bungalow, boathouse and wharf for this noted sportsman, naturalist and collector of marine specimens. The firm was again commissioned in 1926; Vanderbilt's second marriage in 1927 ushered in an extensive remodeling program. This second building phase saw the erection of the Marine Museum to house its owner's expanding collection, the extensive remodeling of the main house in the "Spanish" style to enclose three sides of a central courtyard and the impressive entrance tower. A third building phase resulted in the Memorial Wing, designed by Ronald H. Pearce and built ca. 1935 in memory of Vanderbilt's son, who had been killed in an automobile accident in 1933. Today, "Eagle's Nest"'s stucco walls, tile roof, wrought-iron window grilles and balcony railings, courtyard cloister and prominent bell tower evoke a Spanish Colonial ambience. When Vanderbilt died in 1944, the property was donated to Suffolk County to serve as a museum of natural history. (CT) *112: A view of ca. 1928. 112A: The bell tower, seen from the courtyard.*

113. ALUMINAIRE HOUSE

New York Institute of Technology, Central Islip Campus, Carleton Avenue, Central Islip (in process of restoration). This experimental prototype house was originally built by architects Kocher & Frey to exhibit at the Architectural and Allied Arts Exposition in New York City in 1931. Sheathed in corrugated aluminum panels, it was an early example of Machine Age prefabrication — all of its parts could be screwed together like pieces of an erector set. One of its designers, Albert Frey, had worked with Le Corbusier in France before coming to America. The house was moved to Wallace K. Harrison's estate in Huntington, where it served as a guest house for many years. In recent years it has been moved once again to a new site on the Central Islip Campus of New York Institute of Technology. (AG)

114. "WAWAPEK FARM," ROBERT W. deFOREST HOUSE

Shore Road, Cold Spring Harbor (private residence — not open to the public). Situated on a hill overlooking the harbor and village of Cold Spring Harbor, the mansion was built in 1898 for corporate lawyer and philanthropist Robert Weeks deForest, who adopted the Indian name for the area for his country home. DeForest was also a champion of conservation, and his familiarity with the Adirondacks is evident at "Wawapek" in its rustic lodge-like quality and first story of large, smooth-faced stones laid in a random fashion. Combining elements of the Shingle Style and Colonial Revival into an overall eclectic design, the second and third stories are shingled, and the dominant feature of the entrance facade is the recessed two-story porch behind a screen of classical columns. Designed by the young Grosvenor Atterbury, who would later distinguish himself as the architect of such large housing projects as Forest Hills Gardens, the angled plan of the house follows a curve in the hill. Still in family hands today, "Wawapek" survives largely in its original form. (CT)

115. "BURRWOOD," WALTER JENNINGS ESTATE

Private Road, Cold Spring Harbor (private — not open to the public). Occupying a magnificent site overlooking Cold Spring Harbor and Long Island Sound, "Burrwood" was built in 1898 for Walter Jennings, a director of the Standard Oil Co. from 1903 to 1933, by the prominent architectural firm of Carrère & Hastings. "Burrwood" derives its name from Aaron Burr, one of Mr. Jennings' illustrious, if ill-fated, ancestors. The brick hip-roofed Georgian mansion was inspired by Georgian manorhouses that Jennings saw while on a tour of England. White marble trim surrounds the major windows on the second story and extends down to frame the doorway. The interior is noteworthy for elaborate imported marble mantels, decorative wood paneling and painted wall panels depicting the Eight Wonders of the World. In 1950 the Industrial Home for the Blind acquired the house on 35 acres and surprisingly few alterations were made. The house, formerly the Industrial Home for the Blind, but now a private residence again, remains remarkably intact and in command of its site. (CT) *115: The east facade, 1976. 115A: The east facade, 1929.*

115

115A

Cold Spring Harbor

116

116. ST. JOHN'S CHURCH

Route 25A, Cold Spring Harbor (Laurel Hollow; accessible to the public). St. John's Church was erected in 1835 by architect-builder Smith Sammis near the west end of the Cold Spring Harbor milldam on land acquired from John H. Jones. The church was incorporated the following year in the same month as the Cold Spring Harbor Whaling Company, founded by John H. and Walter R. Jones. Over half of the founders of the church were also members of the prominent Jones family. A New England Colonial-style shingled structure with arched windows (several containing stained glass by the Tiffany Studios), the church, with its spire-topped octagonal lantern atop a square base, has stood for over 150 years as a beacon to sailors and a landmark to inhabitants of Long Island's North Shore towns and villages. (ELW)

117. "OHEKA," OTTO H. KAHN ESTATE

Avery Road, off Jericho Turnpike, Cold Spring Harbor (private residence — not open to the public). Designed in 1917, this formal Châteauesque estate made an elegant country home for the urbane, German-born financier and railroad man Otto H. Kahn. Delano & Aldrich, Beaux-Arts–trained partners who were once draftsmen in the office of Carrère & Hastings, specialized in stately houses and were known for a regularity of plan and refinement of detail distinct from the more exuberant work of the previous generation of country-house architects. The towered, turreted and stone-walled château sits atop a man-made hill in a landscape designed by the Olmsted Brothers. The long tree-lined driveway led to an enclosed cobbled court on the building's east side, while a grass terrace opened onto the west. A similar terrace on the south overlooked formal gardens and an amphitheater. From 1948 through 1979 "Oheka" housed the Eastern Military Academy. Restored by Gary Melius in 1983, it is now a private residence, reputedly the largest in the country. (EF) *117: A view of 1924. 117A: A view of 1976 before restoration.*

117

117A

Cold Spring Harbor

89

B

C

A

THE COLD SPRING

Upper and Lower Bungtown Roads, Laurel Hollow

*T*he Cold Spring Harbor Laboratory is situated on 100 park-like acres in the Incorporated Village of Laurel Hollow, on the western shore of Cold Spring Harbor. An independent research institution with a world-class reputation, it began nearly 100 years ago as the Biological Laboratory, established by the Brooklyn Institute of Arts and Sciences in 1890. At first, the laboratory was a seasonal enterprise, but not long after its founding it gained a new year-round neighbor, the Station for Experimental Evolution, which the Carnegie Institute of Washington set up in Cold Spring Harbor in 1904. For many years the Biological Laboratory and the Station for Experimental Evolution were both headed by the noted evolutionist Charles Benedict Davenport. The two laboratories formally became one entity, the Cold Spring Harbor Laboratory, in 1963.

As the laboratory complex evolved, successive building campaigns utilized the architectural expertise of such leading practitioners as Kirby, Petit & Green; H. H. Saylor; Clinton Mackenzie; Peabody, Wilson & Brown; and Charles W. Moore and his collaborators, the firm known as Centerbrook. Today the complex comprises 33 buildings designed in a variety of styles, with several dating from the era of the Cold Spring Harbor Whaling Company (1838–59).

Charles B. Davenport House. The pumpkin-colored Victorian residence at the entrance to the Laboratory, for many years the home of Director Charles B. Davenport, was built in 1884 for the first director of the Fish Hatchery, Frederic Mather. Though furnished with Queen Anne–style windows and embellished with Stick Style detailing on its matching front and rear towers, the house has a center-hall floor plan — very conservative for its date. Used today as a residence hall for scientific staff, Davenport House was restored in 1980 and repainted in colors to match the original.

Oliver and Lorraine Grace Auditorium. This award-winning building, designed by the architectural firm of Centerbrook in 1986, is stylistically well sited within the

D

A: Map of Cold Spring Harbor Laboratory.
B: Davenport House. C: Grace Auditorium.
D: Carnegie Library. E: McClintock Laboratory.
F: Blackford Hall. G: Jones Laboratory.

HARBOR LABORATORY

context of the varied earlier buildings at the Laboratory — its color palette echoes the dark trim on the 1884 Davenport House across the road and its masonry veneer recalls the brick trim on the turn-of-the-century Carnegie Institute buildings near the water. In winter, the tall main dormer window directs thermal energy onto the trombe wall of masonry which forms the south wall of the 375-seat auditorium. Present-day home to the world-famous Cold Spring Harbor Symposium on Quantitative Biology, the Grace Auditorium received the AIA's Archi Design Award in 1987.

Carnegie Library. Although it looks just like an ivy-covered library, in Renaissance Revival style, and in fact functions as the main library of the Cold Spring Harbor Laboratory, this masonry structure was designed by the noted firm of Kirby, Petit & Green in 1905 as the Main Building of the Carnegie Institute's Station for Experimental Evolution.

Barbara McClintock Laboratory. McClintock Laboratory, renamed in honor of the Nobel Prize–winning scientist, was the second of the research laboratories erected by the Carnegie Institute. Patterned architecturally after the original prototype for all subsequent seaside laboratories of experimental evolution — the Stazione Zoologica founded in Naples, Italy in 1873 — the building was erected in 1914. The architectural similarities include Palladian style recessed entrances behind double-height loggias, slightly projecting end bays and parapeted rooflines. The building's architects, Peabody, Wilson & Brown, emphasized these details by the use of brick trim against pale stuccoed walls.

Eugene G. Blackford Memorial Hall. Blackford Hall is one of the earliest examples on Long Island of the residential use of reinforced concrete. Designed by Gardner & Howes, one of New York City's leading practitioners of this "fireproof" method of construction, the building was named after Eugene Blackford, who, prior to joining the Laboratory's Board of Managers, was the Fisheries Commissioner of the State of New York.

John D. Jones Laboratory. The oldest scientific building erected by the Biological Laboratory was named after one of the laboratory's founders, John Divine Jones, a Cold Spring Harbor native who had risen to prominence as the president of the Atlantic Mutual Company. Mr. Jones donated both the lands and the cost of the new laboratory building, which was designed by Lindsay Watson in 1893. Shaped like an old-fashioned schoolhouse, with a cupola on top of its steep hipped roof, the shingled frame building originally contained teaching laboratories for summer courses in biology. Still used for teaching, Jones Laboratory has been renovated for state-of-the-art work in neurophysiology. The award-winning scheme of Charles Moore Associates called for insertion of individually climate-controlled cubicles, clad in aluminum, inside the beaded-board interior shell of the original structure. (ELW)

E

F

G

118

118. "OLD HOUSE" (BUDD–HORTON HOUSE)

East Main Street, Cutchogue (open to the public: 734-7122). One of Long Island's oldest documented dwellings, the Budd–Horton house represents a medieval English house type transplanted to the East End by settlers in the seventeenth century. The so-called "Old House" may date as early as 1649, the year that John Budd left New Haven to join the Southhold community. Budd's daughter Anna married Benjamin Horton, who employed his brother Joshua to reconstruct the house for him in nearby Cutchogue a decade later. The structure later descended in the Wickham family until its forfeiture after the Revolutionary War. It was converted for use as a barn in the nineteenth century. It became the property of the Congregational Society of Cutchogue in 1939 and was restored by architect James Van Alst in conjunction with Southold Township's tercentenary. The structure is of the center-chimney type, with two principal rooms occupying each of the two stories. Remarkable early features that are intact or on view in the present structure include a complete casement-window assembly with leaded glass, the clustered brick chimney and beveled oak clapboards that are characteristic of seventeenth-century house construction. The house is maintained by the Cutchogue–New Suffolk Historical Society and is open to the public May through October. (ZS)

119. FLEET–KENDRICKS HOUSE

New Suffolk Road, Cutchogue (private residence — not open to the public). Cutchogue's much-traveled Fleet–Kendricks House was moved twice before settling at its present location. The dwelling of ca. 1680, originally located on the south side of Main Road in Cutchogue, was built by Joshua Wells, son of William Wells, a founder of Southold credited with the purchase of Cutchogue, Mattituck and Riverhead from Indians. The one-story, five-bay dwelling is topped by a gambrel roof that is a local variant of the Cape Cod style, a common settlement-period house type derived from English rural dwellings. The gable-roof dormers with rounded upper sash and the Federal-style entry are later additions, possibly part of a renovation of ca. 1815. (KB)

120. THOMAS MOORE HOUSE

Main Road, Cutchogue (open to the public: 765-5500). Famous as the site of the meeting in November 1673 between Southold officials and Dutch commissioners hoping to claim dominion over eastern Long Island, the house was built prior to 1658 by Thomas Moore, a founder of Southold who had been born in Southwold, England. Moore's route from England to eastern Long Island by way of Massachusetts was a common settlement pattern for this region. Typical of the First Period Cape Cod house form on the North Fork, the one-and-a-half-story, five-bay dwelling was built around a central chimney boasting four fireplaces. The paneled front door with transom is a modest Georgian addition. The Moore House, restored to its 1790 appearance, is now part of a museum complex that includes a nineteenth-century carriage house and blacksmith's shop, administered by the Southold Historical Society and Museum. (KB)

119

120

Cutchogue

93

121.

121 & 122. CLINTON ACADEMY AND TOWN HOUSE

151 Main Street, East Hampton (museum — open to the public: 324-6850). The brick ends, gambrel roof and belltower distinguish this prominent structure. Named for Gov. George Clinton, the academy opened on New Year's Day 1785, and was the oldest state-chartered academy. Students learned such practical subjects as surveying, navigation and accounting in addition to the classics. Gentleman-architect Samuel Buell designed the building in 1784 and was the institution's first principal. By the late nineteenth century, when statewide public education superseded the academy system, the building was renovated for use as a public entertainment hall. In 1886, the noted architect James Renwick, Jr. designed a new addition for plays, concerts and lectures. The recognition of the architectural significance of the former academy building prompted local residents to restore the building for use as a museum in 1921. Architects John Custis Laurence and Joseph Greenleaf Thorp supervised the removal of the Renwick-designed addition and the restoration of the original building. Today, Clinton Academy is used by the East Hampton Historical Society for community-history exhibits. Adjacent to the academy, and also maintained by the East Hampton Historical Society, is the Town House, unique among Long Island buildings as the only extant town-government meeting place to survive from the Colonial period, having been erected between 1731 and 1734. It may also be the oldest schoolhouse on Long Island, since this was a secondary function of the building. Today it is used for an interpretive exhibit of period school furnishings and accessories. (JAG)

122

123

123. "TOAD HALL"

East Hampton (private residence — not open to the public). One of the most celebrated American residences of the 1980s, "Toad Hall" in East Hampton was designed by Charles Gwathmey and Robert Siegel, in conjunction with Bruce Nagel, in 1983. Laid out on an axis from land to sea, the dynamically complex International Style house appears to be comprised of multiple geometric forms at once united and tied by the encompassing frame of the sunscreen. The artistry of the architects, who have won over 45 design awards, is also seen in the attention to detail and integration of interior and exterior spaces. "People tend to recognize our designs," Gwathmey has stated, "for our architectural principles in working with space, light and circulation are constant." (RBM)

124. EAST HAMPTON FREE LIBRARY

159 Main Street, East Hampton (open to the public). In 1911, a benefactor purchased the Main Street site and commissioned Princeton-trained Aymar Embury II to design a home for the 14-year-old East Hampton Free Library. Embury, later to become one of New York's most renowned architects of bridges and park structures (the Triborough, Whitestone and Henry Hudson bridges were all his designs) submitted three alternative sketches for the Library. The deep-roofed, half-timbered Jacobean building, with its casement-windowed oriels and eyelid dormers, was altered several times from the 1930s through the 1970s. Later in his life, Embury apparently regretted the selection of the English vernacular design, explaining that he "rather regretted the introduction of this note . . . on the village green." (EF)

124

125

125. JOHN F. ERDMAN HOUSE

Lily Pond Lane, East Hampton (private residence — not open to the public). Surgeon John Erdman had this house built in the heart of East Hampton's summer colony in 1913, to the design of Harrie T. Lindeberg of the New York firm of Albro & Lindeberg. Its characteristic "Lindeberg roof" (a 1927 replacement of the original) dominates the Elizabethan-vernacular house, sweeping broadly over the main block and wings and undulating luxuriously over dormers and porch. Other details characteristic of Albro & Lindeberg (who designed four houses on Lily Pond Lane during their 1906–13 partnership) include the use of a single material (in this case beach-sand stucco) for the exterior wall surface, and the grouping of windows into clusters. (EF)

126. FLINN HOUSE

East Hampton, (private residence — not open to the public). As if to meet head-on with the ocean breakers that it faces, the 3000-square-foot Flinn house sweeps southward like a cresting wave. Although in silhouette the house is pure nineteenth-century, with its steeply pitched roof and dominant chimney mass, it is never suffocated by historic cribbing and has to be one of the most successful adaptations of the Shingle Style vernacular to contemporary use anywhere. Designed in 1978 by Jaquelin Robertson, architect and urban planner and a founder of the New York City Urban Design Group, the Flinn House was the second of three important houses that Robertson designed on the East End. The first was the Seltzer House in Sagaponack in 1965 and the third and most recent was the Rose House of 1986 in East Hampton. (AG)

127. GUILD HALL

158 Main Street, East Hampton (open to the public: 324-0806). Guild Hall, a museum-and-theater complex built in 1931, is an expression of the artistic and cultural side of East Hampton's summer community. The Main Street site and the building, designed by Aymar Embury II, were the gifts of Mrs. Lorenzo Woodhouse, whose restoration of the Clinton Academy required the demolition of a wing that had housed an auditorium for cultural events. Embury, an East Hampton summer resident, was nearing the height of his career as an architect of public and residential buildings and as architectural consultant to New York City's Department of Parks under Robert Moses. Guild Hall has a long, simply detailed one-story facade on Main Street, centered by a triple-arched entrance screening a taller auditorium with a cupola-capped polygonal roof. A wing designed by Arthur Newman of Bridgehampton enlarged Guild Hall in 1971. (EF)

126

127

East Hampton

98

128. HOOK WINDMILL

North Main Street, East Hampton (open to the public: 324-4150). The Hook Windmill was built by Eastern Long Island's most active millwright. Between 1795 and 1811, Nathaniel Dominy V built six wind-powered gristmills and three wind-powered sawmills. The other Dominy mills still standing are those on Shelter and Gardiners Islands and the Gardiner Windmill in East Hampton. The Dominy family of craftsmen is also known for the fine furniture and clocks it produced. Nathaniel Dominy V brought the smock mill with all-wooden components to its greatest sophistication. The 1806 Hook Windmill is an excellent example of Dominy's skill as a millwright. Systems of wooden gears power two pairs of millstones, revolve the cap and power many auxiliary machines to transport and process the grain. Among the labor-saving devices in the Hook Windmill are a sack hoist, a grain elevator, a screener to clean the grain and bolters to sift the flour and cornmeal. The Hook Windmill is now operated as a museum by the Village of East Hampton. (RH)

129. "HOME SWEET HOME"

14 James Lane, East Hampton (open to the public: 324-0713). So-called because of its association with the nineteenth-century playwright John Howard Payne, who wrote the famous song text for his opera *Clari*, "Home Sweet Home" is a transitional lean-to type house that preserves significant detailing of its early eighteenth-century construction period. Like its neighbor to the north, the Mulford House (1680, *see* No. 133) "Home Sweet Home" combines the overscaled and chamfered framing of First Period work with applied wood paneling and a decorative shell-carved corner cupboard in the parlor which appear to be of later installation. Its kitchen lean-to is original to the building, however, suggesting that the house itself belongs to a later generation than that which produced the earlier house type, which lacked this feature. Architectural ties with Rhode Island work of the early eighteenth century may also be discerned in the round-headed paneling and pilasters of the parlor wall and in the plaster covered cornice beneath the front-roof overhang. "Home Sweet Home" is owned and administered by the Village of East Hampton, and its grounds include the 1804 Pantigo windmill, moved to the site from the village green. (ZS)

130

131

130. JEWISH CENTER OF THE HAMPTONS

44 Woods Lane, East Hampton (accessible to the public). One of the most celebrated buildings by Bridgehampton's talented Norman Jaffe is the Jewish Center of the Hamptons. Completed in 1988, the East Hampton synagogue received both Long Island and New York State AIA laurels as well as the Award of Merit of the Interfaith Forum on Religion and Architecture. It is characterized on the exterior by its shingle-clad juxtaposed gables; the cedar-lined sanctuary within was designed to evoke Judaic themes. Awash with light streaming from a series of glazed roof panels, the sanctuary emits a sense of peace and tranquility and represented a design challenge that Jaffe called "the most important responsibility I ever had." (RBM)

131. LEWIS HOUSE

East Hampton (private residence — not open to the public). This house, designed in 1953, was the first of several important East End projects by architect Robert Rosenberg, who moved his practice to East Hampton from New York City in the 1950s. He excelled in the small, affordable weekend house designed in the Modernist spirit. His design for the Lewis House in Springs, East Hampton, a small glass box built on posts to raise it above the high tidal waters of its site, was much publicized at the time and became a strong representative image of the ideal escape house of the 1950s. It was on the cover of the July 1954 issue of *American Home* magazine. (AG)

132. MAIDSTONE CLUB

Old Beach Lane, East Hampton (private club — not open to the public). The Maidstone Club's third building stands on the dunes at the foot of Old Beach Lane, the rhythmically massed stucco structure a severe version of a vernacular French farmhouse. Founded as a social sports organization in 1891, the Maidstone Club built first one, then another clubhouse on the uplands. After the second house burned in 1921, New York architect Roger H. Bullard was hired to realize the directors' dream of a casino on the dunes. With its sweeping shingled roofs, hipped turrets and projecting gables, the building's skyline conforms to the undulation of the dunes, the wings at either end rising gradually to the main ridge. The Maidstone Club was remodeled in 1953 by Aymar Embury II. (EF)

132

HAMPTONS STYLE

A

*T*he Hamptons, on Long Island's South Fork, have long been a testing ground for new ideas in domestic architecture. Since the landscape is flat and everything man-made is exposed, nonindigenous forms of architectural expression have always tended to be self-enclosed independent entities, quite often exclamatory and exaggerated in their efforts to stand out. By the 1920s Modernism had started to make its foothold in the area and, in the years immediately after World War II, the East End experienced a flowering of small experimental beach houses by such architects as Peter Blake, Robert Rosenberg and Andrew Geller.

The 1960s saw the emergence of perhaps the single most influential phase of Hamptons architecture when houses by Gwathmey, Siegel; Richard Meier; Julian and Barbara Neski and others came to define the very essence of a new beachfront lifestyle. Characterized by multiple sun decks, large expanses of glass, skylights and simple, bold geometric forms in the tradition of Le Corbusier's early houses, they began to proliferate along beaches and in the middle of the area's many potato fields. This period in turn was followed by a Post Modern sensibility that grew more out of a respect for local building traditions, with many well-publicized examples by architects such as Robert A. M. Stern, Jaquelin Robertson and Robert Venturi. Unfortunately, just as the sixties style of Modernist beach house became redundant and badly replicated, so too were inferior derivative versions of the Post Modernists. Built with none of the understanding and sense of composition that the originators of the style brought to it, this neotraditional style of house became as much a status symbol in the boom years of the Reagan eighties as the Mercedes Benz and clothing by Ralph Lauren. While the rate of change and experimentation has slowed noticeably in recent years as the area appears to be turning more into a year-round, suburban type of community, the Hamptons still remain a place where innovative ideas in architecture are regularly previewed. (AG)

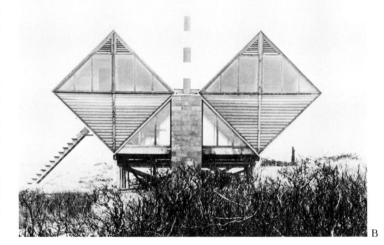

B

C

A: Hoffman House (1966–67), East Hampton, by Richard Meier & Partners. B: Pearlroth House (1959), Westhampton Beach, by Andrew Geller. C: Cohn House (1973), Amagansett, by Gwathmey & Henderson. D: House designed by Julian and Barbara Neski. E: House (1980–83), East Hampton, by Robert A. M. Stern Architects. F: Ertegun House (1989), by Jaquelin Robertson.

D

E

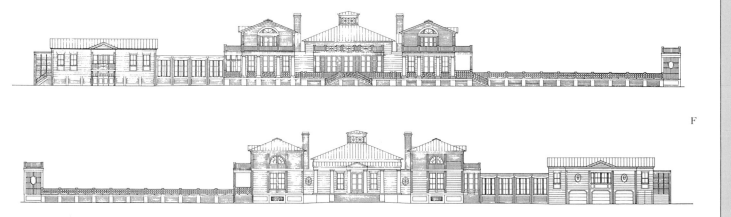

F

103

133

133. MULFORD HOUSE

5 James Lane, East Hampton (open to the public: 324-6850).
Built ca. 1680 for Josiah Hobart (1634–1711), High Sheriff of
Suffolk County, the Mulford House survives as the best-preserved
seventeenth-century house in East Hampton. The original structure was distinguished by a pair of front facade gables, a detail
found on no other First Period Long Island house. Also noteworthy are the finely crafted garret rafters and collar beams that are
embellished with chamfers terminating in lamb's tongues. Two
major renovations were carried out by the Mulford family,
ca. 1720 and ca. 1750, which transformed the original two-story
structure into the present saltbox form with north lean-to. However, many seventeenth-century architectural details survive, such
as the distinctive summer beams in the west parlor and bedchamber. Today, the Mulford House is operated as an architectural-
study house museum by the East Hampton Historical Society.
Exhibits explore architectural history, interior design and decorative furnishings, and the cultural history of the people who lived in
the house for over 250 years. (JAG)

134. SALZMAN HOUSE

East Hampton (private residence — not open to the public).
Along with the Gwathmey house of 1965 in Amagansett, the
Richard Meier–designed Salzman house is one of the most familiar architectural touchstones of Sixties Modernism. Designed in
the spirit of the early pared-down white houses of Adolf Loos and
Le Corbusier, it floats across a pristine lawn like a Modernist ghost
ship. (AG)

134

135. THEODOROS STAMOS HOUSE/STUDIO

1400 Aquaview Avenue, East Marion (private residence — not open to the public). Something like a canary-yellow spaceship raised on a girdle of white posts, this 1959 house was originally built as the home and studio of the Abstract Expressionist painter Theodoros Stamos. Architect/sculptor Tony Smith also designed a house and studio in nearby Southold for the art dealer Betty Parsons. All of Smith's starkly geometric architectural work of this period seems to have presaged his later career as a full-time sculptor. (AG)

136. TUTHILL–SCHAFER HOUSE

Route 25, East Marion (private residence — not open to the public). Erroneously attributed to local carpenter Amon Tabor III, the Tuthill–Schafer House was built in the early nineteenth century, some 60 years after Tabor's death. Perhaps a descendant of Tabor's built this unpretentious house for Harmon Tuthill, who counted among his ancestors Henry Tuthill, one of the founders of Southold. This vernacular house is typical of the Long Island "half-house" form: three bays wide with a side hall entrance. The Greek Revival detail is modest, apart from the main entry, which celebrates the style with carved rosettes, pilasters and Ionic columns. Unusual and possibly added later are the blue transom glass and bosses of the same material on the door casing. Elaborate doorways in the Greek Revival style grace a number of nineteenth-century buildings in East Marion. (KB)

137

137. SMITH–ROURKE HOUSE

350 South Country Road, East Patchogue (private residence — not open to the public). This large and impressive Greek Revival dwelling (ca. 1837), which remains in private ownership, exemplified the restrained massing and architectural detail associated with the region. Its distinctive cupola, decorative porch columns and elaborate paneled front door, however, all reveal the unknown builder's familiarity with contemporary architectural trends. The two-story structure preserves such original features as narrow wood clapboards and operable shutters, four symmetrical chimneys centered within each of the principal rooms, denticulated cornices and a modified Gothic motif surrounding each window. Built by Captain William Smith, Jr., a seaman-farmer associated with the noted "Tangier" Smith clan of nearby Shirley, the house was acquired by Charles Rourke in 1864. A carriage barn of the mid-nineteenth century remains standing on the property. (ZS)

138. JOSEPH BREWSTER HOUSE

East Main Street (Route 25A and Brewster Lane), East Setauket (open to the public: 751-2244). Celebrated as one of the archetypal "Long Island Farmhouses" shown in a painting of that title executed by William Sidney Mount in 1862, the Joseph Brewster House incorporates the sweeping roofline, oversized shingles and compact gable wall that characterize Long Island dwellings of the early to mid eighteenth century. The internal plan is complex, however, having evolved through at least four stages of construction, the last of which was the south addition with the chimney that appears in the Mount view. Believed to have been first built as a single, six-post frame of one-story height ca. 1700, the structure descended in the Brewster–Davis family until its acquisition for preservation by Ward Melville in 1948. Restoration was undertaken in 1967, at which time the house was designated an architectural-study house and subsequently conveyed to the Stony Brook Community Fund, which administers the property today. (ZS) *138A: The house as painted by Mount in 1862.*

138

138A

East Setauket

107

139

140

East Setauket / Farmingville

139. SHERWOOD–JAYNE HOUSE

Old Post Road, East Setauket (open to the public by appointment: 941-9444). Surrounded by sheep pastures, orchards and woodland, the Sherwood–Jayne House in East Setauket is one of several significant Long Island landmarks that are owned and administered by the Society for the Preservation of Long Island Antiquities. Once the country home of Society founder Howard C. Sherwood, the house is a center-chimney, two-story dwelling of ca. 1730 with an added lean-to that gives the end gable wall its distinctive saltbox profile. Enlarged in the eighteenth century and again in the early twentieth, the house preserves original doors, fielded paneling and chimneypieces that are characteristic of early craftsmanship. Unusual freehand wall paintings that date from the early nineteenth century may be seen in the parlor and bedchamber and are associated stylistically with contemporary Connecticut work. The house was acquired in 1908 from Miss Lillie M. Jayne, a lineal descendant of the builder, and was a bequest of Mr. Sherwood to SPLIA in 1957. It is open to the public by appointment from June to October. (ZS)

140. KIAULENAS HOUSE

46 Linden Lane, Farmingville (private residence — not open to the public). Vassia and Laura Kiaulenas, a mother and daughter who are both architects, not only designed their remarkable house at Farmingville, they built it after their contractor died. The ten-year effort that commenced in 1959 produced a dramatic neo-Expressionist residence on a trapezoidal plan that the *Architectural Record* hailed as "an individual expression of strength and integrity" (February 1973). Situated on a wooded knoll with distant views of Long Island Sound, the entire structure is formed from just twelve major beams and the soaring chimney. (RBM)

141. FIRE ISLAND LIGHTHOUSE

Fire Island National Seashore, Fire Island (open to the public: 321-7028). The Fire Island Lighthouse, the tallest on Long Island, was built in 1858 to serve as the first landfall for transatlantic ships bound for New York. The brick tower, 140 feet tall, carried a first-order Fresnel lens, the largest and most powerful of a new optic then being introduced into American lighthouses. The conical tower was distinguished by architectural embellishments not common to lighthouses. Many of these, including brick pilas-ters with granite caps around the neck of the tower, were later obscured when the tower received a covering of concrete. The lighthouse was in poor condition when it was abandoned by the U.S. Coast Guard in 1973. The Fire Island Lighthouse Preservation Society began an effort to restore the lighthouse in 1982. The 1859 double keepers' dwelling is now a museum and restoration of the tower is under way. (RH)

142

143

142. PLATT HOMESTEAD

Sunken Meadow Road, Fort Salonga (private residence—not open to the public). An important example of the developed center-hall colonial house type, the 1754 Platt Homestead in Fort Salonga preserves its rural setting on an estuary of Long Island Sound. An early eighteenth-century English barn, a slave cabin and other outbuildings further distinguish the property as a significant survival of not only the main house but also its historic context. Like the Joseph Lloyd Manor House in Lloyd Harbor, with which it may be compared on stylistic grounds, the Platt Homestead retains large principal rooms on each floor arranged around transverse center halls. The center staircase, however, rises from the back of the main hall and is therefore unusual for Long Island work, although precedents may be cited for the plan in contemporary Connecticut houses. The Platt Homestead was built by Zephaniah Platt, a descendant of Richard Platt of Milford, Connecticut. The house was occupied by the Lamb family in the nineteenth century and remains in private ownership. (ZS)

143. GARDINERS ISLAND FARM GROUP

Gardiners Island (private ownership—not open to the public). Gardiners Island, which has remained in family ownership since its settlement in the seventeenth century, preserves a remarkable cluster of farm-related buildings including a windmill, cheese house and mule barn. The earliest in the group is the carpenter shop (ca. 1690), a heavily framed structure composed of two distinct structural units that are sited into an embankment. The smock mill, built by Nathaniel Dominy V in 1795 and rebuilt in 1815, replaced an earlier post mill. Several eighteenth-century barns, a blacksmith shop and quarters for the farm laborers who were imported seasonally from the mainland complete the group. Of particular interest is a two-story corner tower of one such dwelling that is now believed to be an eighteenth-century portable sawmill later incorporated into the present structure. Its battered walls and wooden wheels, concealed behind the foundation, betray its original use and may identify it as the only example of the form surviving today. (ZS)

144

144. "WESTBROOK" (NOW THE BAYARD CUTTING ARBORETUM)

Montauk Highway, Great River (open to the public: 581-1002). Situated on a 635-acre tract overlooking the Connetquot River, "Westbrook," begun in 1886, would eventually include a complete model-farm group, a series of hothouses, a bowling green, tennis courts and a golf course. Designed by New York City architect Charles C. Haight (1841–1917), best known as a designer of institutional buildings, including several at Columbia University, the main house is freely massed Shingle Style structure with Tudor detailing enlivened with transverse gables, eyelid dormers and a two-story semicircular tower topped by a bell-shaped roof. The interior, little altered by its adaptation to public use, features paneling and hand-carved woodwork in the entrance hall and two magnificent Tiffany stained-glass windows highlighting the stair hall. Cutting, a wealthy entrepreneur, was also an amateur devotee of arboriculture and hired Frederick Law Olmsted to landscape the grounds. Particularly interesting is the pinetum, where Cutting brought conifers from all over the world. Donated in trust to the State of New York in 1936 by Cutting's granddaughter, Mrs. Bayard James, the house and most of the grounds are open to the public as the Bayard Cutting Arboretum. (CT) *144: Waterfront facade. 144A: Main entrance.*

144A

Great River

145. EMMANUEL EPISCOPAL CHURCH

Great River Road, Great River (open to the public). Great River's charming Emmanuel Episcopal Church grew by accretion from its modest beginnings as a one-room Carpenter Gothic chapel in 1862. An openwork steeple (since shingled over) and two eight-foot-square wings were added in 1877, while other improvements were undertaken in 1879, 1880, 1908 and 1909. Happily, the well-conceived changes enhanced and complemented the picturesquely massed building, which in the Victorian era was painted in an eye-catching polychromatic scheme. The interior is noteworthy for its early twentieth-century Tiffany window entitled *Christ with Child and Adoring Angels*; several other unsigned windows have also been attributed to the Tiffany Studios. (RBM)

146. BRECKNOCK HALL

North Road, Greenport (private residence — not open to the public). Brecknock Hall was built in 1866 by Richard B. Conklin, a New York provisions dealer who was descended from the Long Island family that traces its lineage to John Conklin (d. 1694) of Southold. Richard B. Conklin practiced first as a carpenter in New York City, then superintended the stageworks of the Italian Opera House, and finally rented a stall at the Fulton Market where he found an outlet for produce grown on the ancestral Southold farm. Retiring from that business in 1862, Conklin returned to the North Fork and built the large, fashionable stone house and barn complex on a site overlooking Long Island Sound to the north of Greenport village. The house, a superb example of the restrained Italianate Revival style, combines bracketed eaves under a low hipped-roof profile with decorative details such as a cupola, projecting center bay with prominent double doors, and a one-story porch stretching across the front facade. The barns were added in 1868 when Conklin began raising thoroughbreds, among them the celebrated Rarus, who held the world's trotting record in 1878 and fetched the sum of $36,000 from an enthusiastic bettor. (ZS)

147. CONKLIN HOUSE

636 Main Street, Greenport (private residence — not open to the public). The Conklin House is one of the earliest buildings on Greenport's Main Street. Beginning in the 1820s, architectural elements taken from the Greek temple form were not only used on prominent public and ecclesiastical buildings, but were also adapted for use on even the humblest domestic structures. The diminutive Conklin House of ca. 1820 is such an American "cottage temple." Here the ancient pediment form is recalled in the front-gable roofline, which terminates in an abbreviated entablature at either end. The piers flanking the door and sidelights match the side pilasters. The bold corners about the door and windows, although unusual, are not unique. They nearly match a similarly scaled house in Sag Harbor. (CO)

148

148. JOHN MONSELL HOUSE

726 Main Street, Greenport (private residence — not open to the public). Located just north of Townsend Manor is one of Greenport's most decorative mid-nineteenth-century residences. Locally known as the "Gingerbread House," and owned by John Monsell ca. 1873, this building represents a highly individualistic handling of Italianate elements by an unknown architect. Wide overhanging eaves are supported on elaborately scrolled brackets. The paired arched windows are embellished with delicately scal- loped trim above and below. Elaborate trim also adorns the origi- nal six-bay side loggia, which is artfully met by a most unusual, undulating front wraparound veranda, probably added ca. 1900, when the house was owned by S. J. Adams. The doorway contains rare dark-red and blue stained-glass windows with cutout stencil-type designs. Although the interior has been completely reno- vated, the exterior, with its profusion of complex detailing, has been beautifully preserved. (CO)

149. TOWNSEND MANOR

714 Main Street, Greenport (accessible to the public). Whal- ing ships sailed out of Greenport from 1829 to 1859, at a time when many of Long Island's prosperous whaling captains found the fashionable Greek Revival style well suited to their taste. Captain Cogswell's residence, now known as Townsend Manor Inn, dis- plays the deep temple-front portico and full pediment that are hallmarks of the style. The crisp linear detailing in the pediment and along the architrave and frieze is in keeping with the bold simplicity of the four square pillars and capitals. Cogswell lived in his stately home only from 1835 until 1849 when he, like many other Long Island seafarers, left for the West Coast during the booming days of the California Gold Rush. (CO)

150. WELLS HOUSE

530 Main Street, Greenport (private residence — not open to the public). Early Italianate buildings were modeled after the farmhouses of northern Italy, with their L- or T-shaped floor plan and distinctive square towers. This Villa Style is well exemplified in the Wells House of ca. 1870. Its tower, with paired arched windows on its upper tier, is capped by the same overhanging bracketed eaves that define the rest of the flat roofline. The stylish arcaded porches and the protruding bay at the south are typical Italianate features. The building is locally known as the Wells House, after the infamous Captain Wells who is reported to have entered the slave trade in an attempt to regain the fortune he lost in unprofitable whaling expeditions. He enlarged his vessel, the *Good Swallow*, and left Greenport for the west coast of Africa, never to be heard of again. It is believed his foreign crew mutinied on the homebound voyage and took the profit for themselves. (CO)

149

150

151

151. THE BIG DUCK

Sears–Bellows Park, Route 24, Hampton Bays (open to the public). A Long Island icon, The Big Duck was built between 1930 and 1931 by the Collins brothers as a roadside stand selling — you guessed it — ducks. It is an example of the commercial architecture of the early automotive age when "the building became the sign" to compete for motorists' attention. Denise Scott Brown and Robert Venturi, in their seminal 1968 essay "A Significance for A & P Parking Lots, or Learning from Las Vegas," suggested that all such buildings whose imagery bespeaks their function be called ducks or decorated sheds. Hence, this famous Flanders landmark (moved to Sears–Bellows Park in 1988) joins such other three-dimensional billboards as the "Big Pump" in Maryville, Mo., the San Antonio Pig and countless giant milk bottles, hot dogs and coffeepots as an American vernacular phenomenon. (RBM)

152. PRIVATE RESIDENCE

Duckwood Road, Hampton Bays (private residence — not open to the public). In the tradition of an earlier generation of Modernist design, this house, built in 1985, is really a machinelike object perched among the trees and swamp grass of its bay-front setting. A starkly minimal facade, accented with a bright red steel overhang to announce the main entrance, conceals an interior richness and complexity that are not usually associated with this sort of severe geometric style. The building was designed by architect Tod Williams, an associate of Richard Meier from 1967 to 1972. The work of his young architectural firm, Tod Williams & Associates (in existence since 1977), has been published extensively and exhibited at The Museum of Modern Art and the Whitney Museum of American Art. (AG)

152

153

153. First Presbyterian Church

Main Street, Huntington (accessible to the public). A classic example of Georgian form and style, the First Presbyterian Church ("Old First") was built in 1784 to replace an earlier church that was occupied and destroyed during the British occupation of Long Island (1779–83). Inspired by the work of the noted English architect Sir Christopher Wren (1632–1723), the form had reached the American colonies in the 1720s but continued to dominate church design until well into the following century. "Old First" is one of the finest of the type left standing in this region. Outwardly restrained in composition and detail, it also embodies the characteristics of Long Island vernacular construction. A two-story rectangular block, the sanctuary recedes behind a narrow,

square tower that soars five stories to an octagonal base supporting the tapered spire. Ornament is sparse, and includes circular window openings at the attic story of the front facade and a single round-arched window in the tower. The entire edifice is sheathed with long wooden shingles—an eighteenth-century Long Island idiom—and the straightforward application of the tower to the boxlike sanctuary behind invites comparison to less formal examples such as the Caroline Church in Setauket of ca. 1729 [see No. 212]. In the Huntington church, however, the tower has become attenuated, its windows integrated into the design, and the overall composition has achieved a refinement of scale and decoration that is lacking in the earlier building. (ZS)

154

155

154. WALLACE K. HARRISON HOUSE

140 Round Swamp Road, Huntington (private residence — not open to the public). A spare white Modernist composition of rectangles and circles makes up the design of this house, built in 1930 for and by the Rockefellers' principal architect, Wallace K. Harrison (1895–1981). The circular shape of the large living room (with a mural by Fernand Léger) is echoed by the shape of a smaller room, the swimming pool and a separate outbuilding that served as Harrison's studio. Beaux-Arts–trained Harrison's roster of major commissions (in association with Max Abramovitz) includes some of the most important institutional and corporate designs since World War II: Rockefeller Center (1941–74), the United Nations Headquarters (1947–53), Lincoln Center for the Performing Arts (1959–66) and the Albany Mall (1963–78). (AG)

155. HUNTINGTON TOWN HALL

227 Main Street, Huntington (private company — not open to the public). Peabody, Wilson & Brown designed Huntington's handsome Georgian Revival Town Hall on Main Street in 1909, creating a dignified seat of government for a population of some 18,000. The symmetrical hipped-roof brick building is centered by a monumental Ionic portico screening an arch-windowed entrance pavilion crowned by a tall, bell-capped clock tower. A few years after its completion in 1911, the journal *Architect* called the building a good example of its style, and praised its designers for their excellent work. In 1980, the town government having long outgrown its 69-year-old headquarters, the building was sold to a private company for use as an office. (EF)

156. JARVIS–FLEET HOUSE

424 Park Avenue, Huntington (private residence — not open to the public). Named in part for Capt. William Jarvis, a whaler-turned-farmer who enlarged the house with a gambrel-roofed main section some time after 1702, the Jarvis–Fleet House may incorporate a small wing built by Richard Latting ca. 1653. The house served as Huntington's first general store after its acquisition by Joseph Langdon in 1736 and continued as such throughout the eighteenth century under the ownership of Joseph Lewis. It was purchased by Samuel Fleet in 1793, by which time it saw new use as the town's first post office. Fleet was not only the postmaster (1811–23), he also served as town supervisor (1814–15) and was the founder of the Huntington Academy, in addition to being a licensed innkeeper. Now a private residence, the structure is architecturally distinguished as a large and remarkable early example on Long Island of the formal, two-story center-hall Colonial house type. (ZS)

157. KISSAM HOUSE

Corner of Park Avenue and Woodhull, Huntington (open to the public: 427-7045). The Kissam House, one of three historic sites owned and administered by the Huntington Historical Society, is technically a two-story "half-house" (i.e., side-hall, three-bay form) with a side wing — a characteristic late eighteenth-century Long Island house type. It is believed that Jonathan Jarvis built the house in 1796 for Dr. Daniel Whitehead Kissam, who practiced medicine in Huntington until his death in 1839. Kissam's son-in-law, Dr. Charles Sturges, continued the practice until the sale of the house in 1857. Having survived unaltered for more than a century, the structure was acquired by the Society in 1967 from the estate of Hilda Taylor. A historic barn from nearby Lloyd Harbor was restored on the property in 1973. Reinstallation of the house occurred in 1985 in accordance with Dr. Kissam's inventory dated 1839, and the structure is now open to the public. (ZS)

156

157

158

158 & 159. SOLDIERS' AND SAILORS' MEMORIAL BUILDING AND TRADE SCHOOL BUILDING

228 Main Street, Huntington (accessible to the public). The area surrounding Huntington's Old Town Hall Historic District developed slowly during the nineteenth century and experienced its first real period of prosperity and development at the turn of the century, when Huntington gained popularity as a fashionable summer resort. During this time the brick commercial buildings were built along Main Street, as well as numerous architect-designed civic structures. Built in 1892 and designed by the prominent firm of Cady, Berg & See, responsible for one of the wings of the American Museum of Natural History (1899), the Soldiers' and Sailors' Memorial Building was one of the first of these buildings heralding the town's new civic pride. The one-story granite Tudor Revival structure, with a steep hipped slate roof and projecting gable-roofed half-timbered entry, served as the town's first library and today houses the offices of the Huntington Town Historian. Also designed by Cady, Berg & See in the Tudor Revival Style is the Huntington Sewing and Trade School across the street at 209 Main Street. This educational facility, erected through funds donated by Miss Cornelia Prime, a prominent local citizen, had 150 students and eight faculty members shortly after it opened in 1900. Today it houses the administrative offices and library of the Huntington Historical Society. (CT) *158: Memorial Building. 159: Trade School.*

159

Huntington

160. BAYBERRY POINT HOUSES

Bayberry Road, Islip (private houses — can be seen from the road). Bayberry Point, a peninsula extending into Great South Bay, was acquired in the 1890s by sugar magnate H. O. Havemeyer, who dug a canal, constructed a bridge and, between 1897 and 1898, built ten summer residences, including his own, in an unusual experiment in cooperative living among the wealthy. Grosvenor Atterbury (1869–1956), the architect of the model development of Forest Hills Gardens, designed four different "Moorish"-style stucco houses with flat roofs and simple wall surfaces that were intended to relate to their open and stark site, with color supplied by tiled roofs of red or green. Asymmetrical massing of rectangular volumes, giving a modern feeling, coupled with occasional arched or rounded windows or doorways, characterize the structures. Landscaping was kept to a minimum, to blend with the natural aspects of the site. Today structural alterations and plantings have obscured much of the original design. A view, ca. 1907 (No. 160), shows the houses as they were originally designed, without vegetation. (CT) *160: A view of ca. 1907. 160A: A modern view.*

161. St. Mark's Church

St. Mark's Lane, Islip (under restoration after a fire). Financier William Kissam Vanderbilt, Sr., one of the first to build a large country house in the Oakdale/Islip area in the 1880s, was the benefactor of St. Mark's Church and commissioned the Vanderbilt family architect, the prominent Richard Morris Hunt (1827–1895), to design this unusual and sophisticated country church. Hunt's inspiration for the building were the early Scandinavian wooden "stave" churches, and he even brought artisans from Norway to help in the construction of the building. The Scandinavian Timberwork Style (also called Norwegian Gothic) is here characterized by projecting gables with detailed carving, exposed framing, decorative timberwork and shingled wall surfaces. The interior includes stained-glass windows, one an early Tiffany window depicting St. John the Evangelist. The nearby Parish House, built in 1890, was designed by the local architect I. H. Green. (CT)

162. "Coindre Hall," George McKesson Brown Estate

Browns Road, off Southdown Road, Lloyd Harbor (not accessible to the public—status uncertain). Architect Clarence Luce designed this tan stucco Châteauesque residence and complex of coordinating outbuildings, built 1910–11, for George McKesson Brown, a member of the family that owned the McKesson Chemical Company in Connecticut. Set on a hill commanding Huntington Harbor, the formally symmetrical hipped-roof house spikes the skyline in a delicate rhythm of conical-capped towers and slender, channeled chimneys. An elaborate window gable breaks the roofline over the center entry, a French Gothic confection rich with ogee arches, clustered colonnettes and scrolled brackets shaped like fantastic plunging fish. Brown lost his mansion in the 1929 stock-market crash, and during its later career as a Catholic boys' school, "Coindre Hall," the house was enlarged and altered. Suffolk County's Parks Department purchased the property in 1973 and has endeavored to maintain the house and grounds, but the future of the entire property is uncertain. An octagonal-towered boathouse on the bay, and a picturesque grouping of servants' quarters and garage featuring a peaked-capped, spired and corbelled tower (severely deteriorated), survive from the original estate. (EF)

163. "ROSEMARY FARM," ROLAND RAY CONKLIN ESTATE
(SEMINARY OF THE IMMACULATE CONCEPTION) [DESTROYED BY FIRE]

West Neck Road, Lloyd Harbor (not open to the public).
"Rosemary Farm," one of the few Long Island country houses designed by the noted Philadelphia architect Wilson Eyre, was commissioned by utilities and land developer Roland Ray Conklin and completed in 1908. Although born in Illinois, Conklin came from a Long Island family which first settled in Southold in 1641. Conklin's great financial success and real-estate acumen enabled him to create a superlative country estate. A rambling red-brick and shingle house with a broad roof and four asymmetrical wings, the house is thought to have been constructed of local West Neck

bricks, taken from an area long known for its natural clay deposits. Adjacent to the main house and now overgrown is a remarkable amphitheater that boasted a moat, stage and artificial waterfall. Set into a wooded hill and designed by the Olmsted Brothers, the amphitheater was the scene of a 1917 charity event to aid the National Red Cross in World War I. The estate was sold to the Brooklyn Diocese in 1924, and a large seminary was constructed on the property in 1930 [*see* No. 171]. Until it was destroyed, "Rosemary Farm" was used as a retreat house. (CT) *163: The east facade, 1976. 163A: A panoramic view of the amphitheater, 1915.*

Lloyd Harbor

164. Charles Homer W. Davis House

381 West Neck Road, Lloyd Harbor (private residence — not open to the public). Retaining the mansard roof, symmetrical tower and bracketed cornices that are associated with its Second Empire style, the Charles Homer W. Davis house near Huntington is a fine example of pre–Civil War domestic design. It is seen here in a rendering of ca. 1880. Still privately owned, the house incorporates such original detailing as iron roof cresting, decorative Victorian mantelpieces and inlaid flooring. Sited on a hill overlooking scenic West Neck Road, the house is approached by a curvilinear driveway that survives from an original landscape plan. Also surviving on an adjacent parcel is the carriage house, now a private residence, that echoes the design of the main house. (ZS)

165 & 166. "Caumsett," Marshall Field Estate & Polo-Stable Complex (now Caumsett State Park)

Lloyd Harbor Road, Lloyd Harbor (open to the public: 423-1770). Marshall Field III, philanthropist, publisher and grandson of the prominent Chicago merchant, was born in the United States but raised in England. Admiring the great Georgian country houses that he saw as a youth, Field turned to John Russell Pope (1874–1937), an architect recognized as a consummate designer of country houses, including 15 on Long Island, to create an American counterpart at Lloyd Harbor. Pope devised a stately Georgian Revival main house, started in 1924 and completed in 1925, reminiscent in style and spirit of Belton House, near London, attributed to Sir Christopher Wren. The polo-stable complex, designed by Pope in association with noted farm-building architect Alfred Hopkins (who also designed the garage and dairy group), boasts double curved Dutch gables and elaborate scrollwork detail. Other estate buildings, encompassing a variety of styles, included winter and summer cottages used as guest houses, a large indoor tennis house by Warren & Wetmore and 21 cottages built to house workers. In fact, during the heyday of the Field ownership, "Caumsett" required over 85 employees to run the 65-room house and 1750-acre estate, much of it a working farm with a prized herd of Guernsey cattle. Used by the Office of War Information during World War II and sold by Field's widow in 1956, "Caumsett" is now owned and administered by the Long Island State Park Region and is listed on the National Register of Historic Places. (CT)

165

166

Lloyд Harbor

125

167

167. ROBERT LEONHARDT HOUSE

Mallard Drive, Lloyd Harbor (private residence — not open to the public). In an unabashedly direct interpretation of Miesian ideas, in 1956 Philip Johnson designed a glass-lined living room that projects boldly out toward the water away from the less-dramatic private areas of the house, which are contained within white brick walls. (AG)

---

168. HENRY LLOYD HOUSE

Lloyd Harbor Road, Lloyd Harbor (open to the public: 424-6110). Henry Lloyd (1685–1763), son of the patentee James Lloyd, was the first of the name to occupy the Manor of Queens Village (now Lloyd Neck). Entries in his record book, which is preserved at the Brooklyn Historical Society, reveal that work on the house began with the manufacture of bricks in March 1711, and that the frame for the dwelling was brought from "Setalcott" (Setauket). The original two-story house was enlarged in 1722 with two lean-tos — one on the back and one on the side — resulting in a hipped corner detail that is unusual for the period. The side lean-to contained the kitchen with a separate chimney.

The house was occupied by successive generations of the Lloyd family throughout the eighteenth and nineteenth centuries, and was home to Jupiter Hammon, a trusted slave and America's first published black poet, whose first work appeared on a broadside in 1760. The Henry Lloyd House became the gatehouse to "Caumsett," the Marshall Field Estate [*see* No. 165], in 1921 and was preserved as such until its conveyance to the State of New York in 1961. It is presently administered by the Lloyd Harbor Historical Society, which has undertaken its restoration and furnishing for public visiting. (ZS)

---

169. JOSEPH LLOYD MANOR HOUSE

Lloyd Lane and Lloyd Harbor Road, Lloyd Harbor (open to the public June to October: 941-9444). Overlooking Lloyd Harbor in a setting that has remained remarkably unspoiled since the eighteenth century is the Joseph Lloyd Manor House, a dignified house preserving the simple elegance that characterizes Long Island workmanship before the Revolution. Completed in 1767 under the direction of Abner Osborne, a Connecticut housewright, the manor was home to Joseph Lloyd, who was descended from James Lloyd (1653–1693), the first Lord of the Manor of Queens Village. While James never inhabited the property, his son Henry built a dwelling nearby in 1711 [*see* No. 168] where Joseph was born and resided until the completion of his own house after his father's demise in 1763.

The essential features of the house remain intact today: a five-bay, two-story center-hall plan with large rooms surrounding the central staircase and interior paneled wainscot, chimneypieces and doors indicative of their eighteenth-century style. Certain architectural elements, in fact, reveal the hand of their Connecticut builder and include the provincial treatment of the southwest chamber fireplace wall and the interior pocket shutters, whereas the long exterior wall shingles are indigenous to Long Island. One unusual feature is the break in floor level between the front and back of the house, evidently intended to separate the service spaces from the formal parlor, bedchambers and other important rooms. Preserved at the turn of the century as a guest house on the "Fort Hill" estate [*see* No. 170], the manor house was given to the Society for the Preservation of Long Island Antiquities by Mrs. Willis D. Wood in 1968. It was restored to its post–Revolutionary War state in 1982 and is one of SPLIA's six historic houses now open to the public. (ZS)

168

169

Lloyd Harbor

127

170

170A

Lloyd Harbor

128

170. "FORT HILL"

Fort Hill Drive, Lloyd Harbor (private residence — not open to the public). Erected on the site of Fort Franklin, a British stronghold during the Revolutionary War that overlooked both Cold Spring and Oyster Bay harbors, "Fort Hill" stands today as a case study in the succession of architectural styles on Long Island's Gold Coast in the late nineteenth and early twentieth centuries. The first generation of building on the site saw the erection in 1879 of a Shingle Style "cottage" designed by Charles Follen McKim of McKim, Mead & Bigelow, of which the principal elevation was dominated by a Châteauesque octagonal tower. The house was sold several decades later to William J. Matheson, pioneer of the synthetic-dye industry in America and founder of the Allied Chemical and Dye Corporation. Mr. Matheson, who had family roots in Scotland, engaged the architectural firm of Boring & Tilton (authors of the Immigration Station design at Ellis Island, New York City) to remodel and enlarge the house in the Tudor Revival style. The original house was virtually totally encased in brick. Matheson's daughter, Anna M. Woods, lived in the house for many years. The public was often invited to enjoy its impressive grounds (the work of J. Clinton Mackenzie), landscaped with weeping beeches and oaks and a formal garden. (ELW) *170: The design for the Shingle Style house of 1879. 170A: The house as remodeled, 1903.*

171. SEMINARY OF THE IMMACULATE CONCEPTION

West Neck Road, Lloyd Harbor (not open to the public). The Seminary of the Immaculate Conception in Lloyd Harbor was dedicated on September 30, 1930, two years after ground had been broken on the project, a dream of Brooklyn's Roman Catholic Bishop Thomas E. Molloy (1885–1956) for a modern facility to house 220 seminarians. The huge Spanish Romanesque basilica-inspired structure was designed by Robert J. Reiley (an ecclesiastical architect who was later responsible for the Immaculate Conception Monastery in Jamaica, Queens), with P. L. Robinson serving as the landscape architect. The seminary is formed around a magnificent 185-foot-long chapel with mosaics by Joep Nicho- las, spectacular wrought-iron work by the Ferro Studios of New York and a great Skinner organ. Below the main chapel are a dozen smaller chapels and the crypt, in which Bishop Molloy and his successors are interred. On the exterior, the salient feature is the great bell tower, which rises to a height of seven stories and can be seen by mariners from miles away. At the request of the neighbors, however, bells were never installed. The plan for this building, in which V-shaped wings spring from each end of a central block, was reportedly based by Reiley on the Westchester Biltmore Hotel. (RBM)

171

172

172. VAN WYCK–LEFFERTS TIDE MILL

Mill Road, Lloyd Harbor (open by appointment only: 367-3225). Of the many documented tidal mills built on Long Island in the eighteenth century, the Van Wyck–Lefferts Tide Mill is one of the few that remain standing and the only example that preserves a significant amount of its original wooden machinery. The structure is a three-story, heavily framed building situated at the edge of a man-made earthen dam that separates Mill Cove Pond from Huntington Harbor. It preserves one wall of original exterior shingling as well as batten doors and shutters from its construction period, 1793–97. Periodic reinforcement of its stone foundation, most recently undertaken under the direction of the Society for the Preservation of Long Island Antiquities (1983), has been necessitated by the erosion of the dry stone underpinnings by harbor tides. The mill operated by capturing tide water, which entered the pond through two wooden gates centered on the dam. As the tide fell, the water was fed back to the harbor through a sluice adjacent to the mill, powering an undershot wheel, which drove the machinery inside the structure. Operation of the tide mill ceased by the turn of the century, when the industry itself was obsolete, and the preservation of the structure was undertaken thereafter by private initiative. Today the tide mill and pond are owned by The Nature Conservancy. (ZS)

173. P. Q. WATSON HOUSE

West Neck Road, Lloyd Harbor (private residence — not open to the public). Popular in France in the late nineteenth century, the Second Empire style is unusual in, but not altogether absent from, the Long Island architectural landscape. The P. Q. Watson House, like several other nearby homes, was remodeled ca. 1865 in this ornate Victorian style, and is an excellent example of the thoroughgoing renovation that took place in the 1860s of earlier, simpler farmhouses. The house was originally built in the eighteenth century; clear evidence of its earlier construction is the heavy, hand-hewn beams with interlocking joints in the basement. The Second Empire mansard roof with dormers was desirable for its stylistic merits but also for the functional full attic story gained by its use. The pavilion and elaborate window surrounds, as well as the Italianate double brackets and corresponding paired columns, are all salient features of the style. (KB)

173

174

174. MANOR OF ST. GEORGE

Smith Road, West Side, Mastic (museum — open to the public). The Manor of St. George encompassed some 20,000 acres of land in the seventeenth century, including the site of the present manor house, which replaces the original, built ca. 1690 on a bluff overlooking the Great South Bay. The tract was Colonel William "Tangier" Smith's reward for his service to the British Crown, and his descendants occupied the land continuously until 1954. The present house was built ca. 1810 to replace the second manor house, which was destroyed by fire during the American Revolution. Its six-bay main block incorporates a cross-gable topping a two-story pavilion centered on the main entry that is distinguished by unusual double-hung sidelights. Attached to the main block is a four-bay, one-story wing that may survive from the earlier manor house. Now comprising 127 acres, the property preserves the remains of Fort St. George, a British supply base for land and sea forces, which was destroyed by local patriots in 1780. The house and land were bequeathed to a charitable trust in 1954 by Miss Eugenie Anne Tangier Smith, and are open to the public. (KB)

175A

175. WILLIAM FLOYD ESTATE

20 Washington Avenue, Mastic (unit of National Park Service, open to the public: 399-2030). Eight generations of Floyd family members, including William Floyd, a signer of the Declaration of Independence, have lived at this site. When Nicoll Floyd first moved to Mastic in the 1720s, he built a two-story shingled wood-frame house, three rooms on each floor, facing south toward the bay. The original framing, indicating a strong Connecticut influence, was designed for easy expansion. As Floyd's wealth and family grew, so did the house. William Floyd, returning after the Revolution, enlarged the house, making it suitable for entertaining such national leaders as Thomas Jefferson and James Madison. In 1857, John G. Floyd, Sr. restyled the front, adding the large porch, cornice and other details in the Greek Revival style. He also remodeled the east wing and built a new wing on the northeast side. John G. Floyd, Sr. also added a wing on the northwest side to help accommodate guests and family members during summer retreats from New York City. The rare and valuable quality of the Floyd house is the extraordinary clarity of its eighteenth- and nineteenth-century history, covering the eight generations who have lived there. (SJD) *175A: Ralph Earle's portrait of William Floyd.*

175

176

176. MATTITUCK OCTAGON

Main Road and Love Lane, Mattituck (private offices — can be seen from the road). Built as a house with an attached store in 1854–55, the Mattituck Octagon is one of eight mid-nineteenth-century octagonal buildings surviving on Long Island. This unusual architectural phenomenon was inspired by the writings of Orson Squire Fowler, a phrenologist who espoused eight-sided buildings as being of the "highest practical utility to man," bringing "cheap, convenient, and superior" dwellings within the reach of more Americans. The Mattituck Octagon is of particular interest in that it retains its original room configuration in which "no space is wasted" since right angles are eliminated. (RBM)

177. ESTÉE LAUDER LABORATORIES

South Service Road and Pinelawn Road, Melville (private office — can be seen from the road). The streamlined Estée Lauder Laboratories building was completed in 1967, the year it received an Archi Award from the Long Island Chapter of the AIA. Designed with unlimited expansion in mind, it doubled in size four years later. Nestled behind earth berms, which mask the extent of this 300,000-square-foot plant, its upper level is clad with white porcelain panels and exhibits a uniform window treatment to facilitate additions. Its architects, Davis, Brody & Associates, the nationally known firm that specializes in educational and corporate architecture, worked on this project in conjunction with Richard Dattner & Associates. (RBM)

178. SAINT LOUIS DE MONTFORT CHURCH

New York Avenue and Miller Place Road, Miller Place (open to the public). A dramatic instance of skyward-reaching Expressionism on Long Island is Saint Louis de Montfort Church at Sound Beach, a 1980 Archi Award–winner designed by Lawrence L. Smith Associates. Cited as "a good solution to a complicated, multi-function program by means of a very simple plan," the building is also innovative in its energy-efficient HVAC system. It is reminiscent of an open-sided tabernacle at a nineteenth-century Methodist campground. Its vast slate roof culminating in a steeple seems to float above the laminated piers that support it, perhaps reminding the congregation, which formed in the 1970s, of the tent in which they had previously held services. (RBM)

177

178

Camp-Meeting Grounds

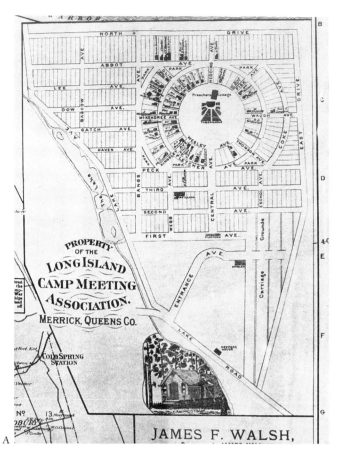

In the nineteenth century, Long Island was a popular location for that American phenomenon, the religious camp meeting. Although several denominations favored the open-air revivals, they were particularly associated with Methodism. As early as 1818, 6000–8000 Methodists, borne by over forty sloops, converged on Cow Harbor (Northport) for such a meeting. After the Civil War, camp-meeting associations were created that sought permanent grounds and facilities, tents gave way to cottages and these seasonal communities proliferated.

In 1871 the Metropolitan Camp Ground Association bought 240 acres at Carpenterville (Sea Cliff) where they had been meeting since at least 1865; the following year the Shelter Island Grove Camp Meeting Association was formed by Brooklyn Methodists; the Long Island Camp Meeting Association first gathered at Merrick in 1868; while the Stony Brook Assembly (site of today's Stony Brook Boys School) was not organized until 1907. Camp meetings also took place at Freeport, Roosevelt and Jamesport, while Point O' Woods on Fire Island was the site of the Long Island Chautauqua Association (1894).

Laid out in circles or squares surrounding a preacher's stand or roofed tabernacle, the camp grounds are still discernible today. Shelter Island Grove had been planned by the Boston landscape architect Robert Morris Copeland, designer of the famous Oak Bluffs campground on Martha's Vineyard and Point O' Woods by Col. John Y. Culver. The surviving cottages, chapels and associated camp buildings in the Carpenter Gothic, Stick, Queen Anne and Colonial Revival styles are among the most exuberant vestiges of Victorian architecture on Long Island. The intricate barge boards (cornices) of Shelter Island Heights' cottages have even led to the local expression "Shelter Island lace," and while the names of the carpenter-builders of most of these cottages are lost to history, it is known that "Honest John" French, a prominent Brooklyn builder and devoted Methodist with a reputation for "mixing mortar with conscience," built the similar cottages east of the ferry dock. French is also thought to have been responsible for the Chapel in the Grove (ca. 1875), or Union Chapel on the Heights, which boasts three remarkably beautiful marine-mosaic memorial windows by the artist Walter Cole Brigham comprised of stone, glass and shell. Sea Cliff's spectacular Wood-Knieriem and Frank Krauss houses are among the region's great architectural treasures from this period. (RBM).

A: Long Island Camp Meeting Association, Merrick, from an 1886 Beers map. B: The Radial plan of the Long Island Camp Meeting Association, Merrick — still visible in 1967. C: Shelter Island Heights. D: Cottage, Shelter Island Grove Camp Meeting Association. E: Union Chapel, Shelter Island Grove.

C

D

E

135

179

179. MILLER–MILLARD HOUSE

North Country Road, Miller Place (open to the public).
Unlike many of its contemporary eighteenth-century dwellings, the Miller–Millard House comprises three distinct units of construction that give it a long, low profile and unique front facade. The center section, which may date from ca. 1720, appears to be the original and survives as the earliest remaining dwelling in Miller Place. The house was enlarged to the west ca. 1750, at which point the front door became a center door and received its elaborate fluted pilasters and pediment. A later east addition, attributed stylistically to the early nineteenth century, completed the plan and gave the house its second front door. Now administered by the Miller Place Historical Society, in the 1970s the house was acquired from a family descendant who had maintained the structure without mechanical systems throughout this century. (ZS)

180. MILLER PLACE ACADEMY

North Country Road, Miller Place (accessible to the public).
Built in 1834, the Miller Place Academy is a late example of the Federal style on Long Island. Designed by rural architect/builder Isaac Hudson, the two-and-a-half-story shingled structure is characterized by simplicity of line and proportion. Decoration is restrained and confined to fine dentil cornices, a fan window in the gable end and an elegant transom-lighted doorway framed by elongated pilasters. When the academy opened, it provided three terms a year for both boys and girls of from ten to 20 years of age. The academy soon established an excellent reputation for the quality of its education and students came from all over the Island to board with local families. It closed its doors in 1868, and the building has since functioned as a public school (1900–37) and free library. In 1976 the Academy was one of 26 structures in Miller Place listed on the National Register of Historic Places. (CT)

180

181

181. MONTAUK POINT LIGHTHOUSE

Montauk Highway, Montauk (museum — open to the public: 668-5340). The first lighthouse on Long Island was built at Montauk Point in 1797 in response to a petition from New York City merchants, who knew that such a light would greatly reduce the hazards of navigation to and from New York Harbor. John J. McComb, Jr., a prominent New York architect and builder, constructed the octagonal sandstone tower that rose 80 feet and carried an iron lantern room utilizing 13 whale-oil lamps. In 1860 the lighthouse was outfitted with a first-order Fresnel lens, an assembly of glass prisms and lenses that stood 12 feet tall and was six feet in diameter. The masonry tower was raised 14 feet to take advantage of the greater range of the new lens. The present double keepers' dwelling was also constructed in 1860. The Montauk Point Lighthouse, automated in 1987, is now operated as a museum by the Montauk Historical Society. (RH)

182. "MONTAUK MANOR"

Edgemere and Essex Streets, Montauk (private apartments — can be seen from the road). Sitting incongruously on Signal Hill, this gargantuan mass of Neo-Tudorism still dominates the high ground of Montauk. Built in 1926 at a cost of $1.5 million, the manor was designed by Schultze & Weaver, the same architects who designed the Waldorf-Astoria (1931) in New York City. The 200-room manor hotel was to be the crown jewel in Carl Fisher's ambitious development project in which he planned to transform Montauk into the "Miami Beach of the North." Fisher's development company went bankrupt in 1934, putting an end to that vision, but the manor has survived the intervening years in relatively good shape, despite the fact that recent condo conversion schemes have altered the building's original elegance. (AG)

182

183

183A

Montauk

138

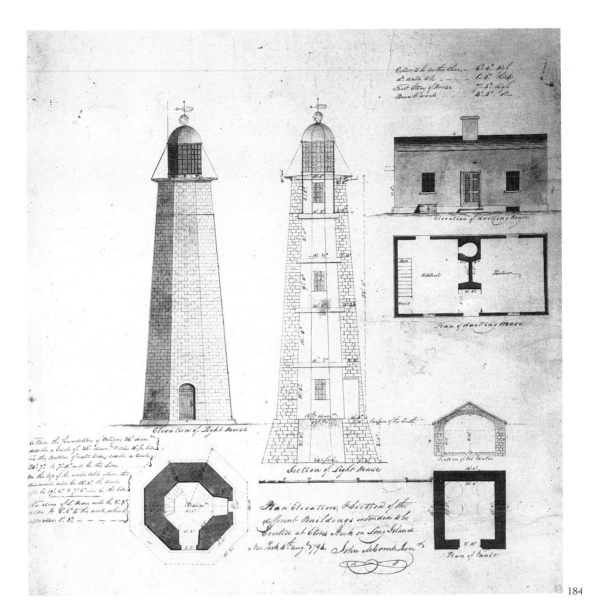

Elevation of Light House

Section of Light House

Plan, Elevation, & Section of the different Buildings intended to be erected at Etons Neck on Long Island. New York 4th Aug.st 1794. John McComb Jun.r

Elevation of dwelling house

Plan of dwelling house

Section of Oil Vault

Plan of Vault

184

183. MONTAUK ASSOCIATION HOUSES

Off Ditch Plains Road, Montauk (private residences — can be seen from the road). The Montauk Association Houses were built between 1881 and 1892 by a group of New York City businessmen as an exclusive sportsmen's club for hunting and fishing in the unspoiled wilds of Montauk. Since all were designed in a similar informal Shingle Style with wide porches, dormers and brick chimneys, there is no one house that stands out with any particular architectural distinction, but taken together they make a very harmonious group. The seven original cottages were set back above the dramatic cliffs of Cottage Point in a flying-wedge pattern to take full advantage of the ocean views and breezes. The positioning of the houses, the layout of driveways and footpaths and the landscaping were by the landscape firm of Frederick Law Olmsted.

In 1879 Arthur W. Benson, a New York financier, had paid $151,000 to purchase the greater part of Montauk. He invited a group of his New York associates and friends to join him in establishing the Montauk Association, and cottages were subsequently designed by McKim, Mead & White for Benson himself, Henry G. deForest, Alexander Orr, Henry Sanger, Alfred M. Hoyt, William L. Andrews and Dr. Cornelius R. Agnew. The Association complex originally included a clubhouse that stood at the center of the property with three houses positioned to the east of it and the other four houses to the west. The clubhouse burned down in 1933. A laundry building and stables also once stood on the property. Other than exterior painting, the houses have undergone only slight alterations since these photos were taken. (AG) *183: The houses in a view of the 1890s. 183A: The Arthur W. Benson House, 1890s.*

184. EATON'S NECK LIGHTHOUSE

Lighthouse Road, Northport. A primary hazard to Colonial shipping in Long Island Sound was a reef off Eaton's Neck. Long Island's second lighthouse was constructed here in 1799 to warn sailors of the reef. John J. McComb, Jr. built the original 50-foot sandstone tower to a design similar to that of the Montauk Point Lighthouse, which he had completed three years earlier. The original drawing is shown here. The height of the tower was raised in 1868 when a third-order Fresnel lens was installed. The light was automated in 1966, but Eaton's Neck is one of the few Long Island lighthouses to retain a Fresnel lens. (RH)

185. "Indian Neck Hall," Frederick G. Bourne Estate (now LaSalle Military Academy)

Montauk Highway, Oakdale (accessible to the public). "Indian Neck Hall" is one of the few surviving South Shore estates. Since 1926, the mansion, coach house, boat house and gate house have all been adaptively reused as part of La Salle Military Academy. Frederick G. Bourne, industrialist, yachtsman and president of Singer Sewing Machine Co., began acquiring land in Oakdale in the 1890s and by 1900 his property comprised 1000 acres. In 1897 he commissioned the noted architect Ernest Flagg to design his estate, which was still being worked on at the time of Bourne's death in 1919. Beaux-Arts–trained Flagg, best known for the Naval Academy at Annapolis and the Singer Building in New York, designed a massive two-and-a-half-story, U-shaped Federal red-brick structure enlivened by marble quoining and a Corinthian-columned portico. Also on the grounds is "Lake House," once the home of Bourne's son Arthur, designed by I. H. Green in 1904. A windmill, once part of the estate and designed by noted farm-group architect Alfred Hopkins, is now in separate ownership. Originally, the estate grounds included a three-mile canal system spanned by a marble bridge that led to a picturesque trout pond. (CT)

186. "Idle Hour," William K. Vanderbilt, Sr. Estate (now Dowling College)

Montauk Highway and Idle Hour Boulevard, Oakdale (open to the public: 589-6100). In 1876, William K. Vanderbilt, soon to become vice-president of the family's New York Central and other railroad lines, commissioned Richard Morris Hunt to design a country estate at Oakdale. That first rambling wooden "cottage" burned in 1899, and was soon replaced by the present 110-room "fireproof" house, designed by Richard Howland Hunt, son of the original architect of "Idle Hour." The estate, now in part the Dowling College campus, included the house itself, a coach house, power house, gate lodges, greenhouses, boat houses and a farm group, many of the structures designed by the Hunts. A number of them have been rehabilitated for modern uses. The Flemish-gabled brick-and-limestone mansion faces the Connetquot River, its L-shaped body sheltering a courtyard with an elaborate "palm garden" at its south corner. (EF) *186: Terrace view, 1903. 186A: The conservatory.*

185

186

186A

Oakdale

141

187

188

187. Terry–Mulford House

Main Road, Orient (private residence — not open to the public). Unique among the East End's earliest dwellings, the Terry–Mulford House near Orient is distinguished as Long Island's only known "plank house." Believed to have been built for Thomas Terry ca. 1672, the house has exterior walls formed of wide, vertical sheathing boards that are trenched into the horizontal framing elements. Traditional construction of the period favored the use of secondary posts and studs, and the appearance of this unusual framing technology continues to puzzle scholars. The house was acquired by Elisha Mulford in 1805 and received additions in the nineteenth century. A later owner, Dr. Henry Heath, added the large two-story wing to the back. Despite local tradition, no documentary evidence confirms the association of the house with John Peakin's Tavern. (ZS)

188. Webb Tavern

Village Lane, Orient (open to the public: 323-2480). Now administered by the Oysterponds Historical Society, the Webb Tavern has been moved twice since its construction in Greenport ca. 1790. While its origins remain obscure, its generic tavern form, with a projecting front-roof sweep and two-story gallery, is physical evidence of its early use as a tavern. Greenport, called Sterling until 1830, developed in the nineteenth century as a summer resort after completion of the Long Island Rail Road. By mid-century, the out-of-date tavern had been moved to the outskirts of town where it served as a dwelling until its acquisition for restoration in 1955. The building was moved by barge to its present site and remains the only example of this architectural form left standing on Long Island. (ZS)

189. PATCHOGUE LACE MILL

West Main Street, Patchogue. At the turn of the century experienced weavers were imported from Nottingham, England, to work the industrial looms at the now-empty Patchogue Lace Mill. The monumental coal-fired complex, covering a 12-acre site, is comparable in size to the vast mills of New England but is unusual for Long Island, which had missed the earlier stages of the Industrial Revolution for lack of falling water to power mill turbines. The complex consists of a number of connected two-story brick buildings highlighted by a traditional mill tower. Built between 1900 and 1906, the mill first produced lace, but later made parachute silk, mosquito netting and gun camouflage when the demand for lace declined. The mill is not only the dominant architectural feature of the area, but was at one time its vital economic force, employing over 900 Patchogue residents until 1954, when it closed. Now standing idle, the complex offers mute testimony to a time when industrial buildings were designed not for function alone but with aesthetics in mind. The buildings are embellished with eye-pleasing detail, notably the elaborate decorative brickwork on the tower and the graceful arches over the second-story window. (KB) *189: The mill, in a contemporary view. 189A. The tower. 189B: A view published on a 1907 postcard.*

189B

189A

190

191

192

190. LENZ VINEYARDS

Main Road, Peconic (open to the public: 734-6010). In contrast to the pretentious winery headquarters that have appeared on Long Island's East End in recent years, the Lenz Winery in Peconic is in touch with its context while appropriately demonstrative of its purpose. Designed by Mark Simon of Centerbrook, who saw the adaptive reuse of the old potato farm as being primarily an exercise in "landscape and exterior reorganization," the recycled farmstead received the Long Island Chapter of the

AIA's Gold Archi Award following its completion in 1982. In symbolic recognition of the vineyard, Simon employed trellises built on top of the same "peeler" poles used as vineyard stakes. "Creating a sense of progression," the fox-grape-covered trellises help define the entrance while separating the public and private areas. The center bay of the large barn serves as the wine-display and tasting room and, to distinguish this trellis-clad structure, two cupolas and a bell tower were added. (RBM)

191. CHURCH OF THE ATONEMENT

Aesop's Neck Lane, Quogue (accessible to the public). Long Island is blessed with a wealth of fine late nineteenth-century ecclesiastical architecture, but Quogue's Church of the Atonement (Episcopal) is an exceptional example of its style and period. Erected in 1884, the Shingle Style church was designed by Sidney V. Stratton in conjunction with McKim, Mead & White, and built

by Mead and Taft of Cornwall-on-Hudson on land donated by prominent parishioner and Quogue summer resident Samuel D. Craig. Cruciform in plan, the concave crossing-tower roof, with its prominent weather vane, juxtaposes with the pinnacled convex dormers to present a picturesque profile. The church also has Tiffany windows. (RBM)

192. CROWELL RESIDENCE AND STUDIO

Quogue (private residence — not open to the public). Mark Simon of the firm of Centerbrook received the Long Island Chapter of the AIA's Gold Archi Award for the Crowell Studio (1984), a composer's retreat on the Quogue shore. While cloaked in East End historicism, with its octagonal domed tower reminiscent of Long Island windmills and lighthouses, the studio is thoroughly

contemporary, making, in its creator's estimation, "no pretense of belonging to any but our own time." A skirt of cedar lattice belies the fact that this house is actually built on poles, the waterfront code requiring the first floor to be 11 feet above sea level. The interior, awash with sunlight, is illuminated by double-hung windows, three "piano key" skylights and a cupola. (RBM)

193

193. "HOLIDAY HOUSE"

Quogue (private residence — not open to the public). The house was built in 1950 as a promotional project for *Holiday* magazine. Its architect, George Nelson, best known for his daring furniture design of the fifties and sixties, used an arrangement of fences, walkways, terraces and open-walled pavilions to create something like a stage set for indoor–outdoor summer living. With its extensive use of motor-controlled lighting, built-in radios, inter-coms, dimmer switches, motorized windows, accordionlike partitions and other domestic gizmos, "Holiday House" epitomized America's love for household gadgetry that blossomed in the 1950s. Other Long Island projects by Nelson of this period (the Woodruff House in Quogue, 1951, and the Johnson House in East Hampton, 1951) proved to be simpler and less expensive experiments in vacation living. (AG)

194. "LONGWOOD"

Longwood Road and Smith Road, Ridge (accessible by special arrangement only). "Longwood" is now a 35-acre farmstead near Ridge that preserves the main house, outbuildings and cemetery of the so-called "Tangier" Smith family, which occupied the property until 1968. The estate was originally part of a Colonel William Smith's (1654/5–1704/5) Manor of St. George [*see* No. 174], a vast expanse of undeveloped land that stretched south from today's Middle Country Road to the Great South Bay. The house was constructed for William Smith, Jr. (1769–1803), a great-grandson of the colonel, who married Hannah Phoenix Smith in 1791. The house is a large, center-hall dwelling that retains such detailing as the front doorway and interior chimneypieces of the Federal period. A major renovation ca. 1850 introduced bracketed eaves and battlements to the roof as well as Gothic Revival chimneys, porches and a privy attached to the back. Still later in the century, ca. 1890, the old kitchen wing was rebuilt as a gambrel-roofed addition with up-to-date kitchen, dining room and spacious bedchambers. Today the estate also includes a schoolhouse relocated from nearby Ridge as well as a large nineteenth-century barn rebuilt on the site of the original, which burned in 1981. "Longwood," acquired by the Town of Brookhaven in 1975, is scheduled to open to the public as a museum complex in the near future. (ZS)

195. RIVERHEAD COUNTY COURT HOUSE

225–235 Griffing Avenue, Riverhead (accessible to the public). America's great legacy of handsome county courthouses is a measure of its respect for temples of justice. Suffolk County's impressive neo-Georgian seat of government with its colossal portico and Corinthian columns, is part of this tradition. Designed by county architect M. Vollney Liddell after a fire destroyed the 1854 court house on April 17, 1927, the stately three-story building (actually a complex of three separate but connected buildings) was completed in 1929. The northernmost component of the complex, the County Clerk's office, was built in 1875 from plans supplied by Tappan Reeve of Brooklyn, and enlarged in 1895 and remodeled after the fire in 1929. The south wing, originally known as the Treasurer's Building, was built between 1916 and 1917. (RBM)

194

195

196

197

196. TRINITY EVANGELICAL LUTHERAN CHURCH

Route 25A, Rocky Point (accessible to the public). Neo-Expressionism seems an appropriate mode for Trinity Lutheran Church, which must compete for the public's attention along a commercial strip of road. Characterized by its soaring copper roof and continuity of form, the house of worship, designed by Edward W. Slater in 1964, is a rare example of the style on Long Island.

Neo-Expressionism became a force in American architecture in the mid-1950s, encouraging architects to express the program or purpose of their structures through dramatically suggestive forms. The most famous local example, Eero Saarinen's TWA Terminal at Kennedy Airport, imitates flight, while Trinity Lutheran expresses a soaring faith. (RBM)

197. EPHRAIM BYRAM HOUSE

Jermain Avenue, Sag Harbor (private residence — not open to the public). This eccentric villa was built ca. 1852 by an inventive man as his own home. Ephraim Byram, born to a family of clockmakers, was a mechanic, astronomer, inventor, bookbinder and cabinetmaker as well as a professional maker of clocks. From the Sherry & Byram Clock Works (which used to stand behind the house) came large clocks destined for steeples and

street posts all along the East Coast. New York's City Hall has a Byram clock, and four were installed in the tower of the Whaler's Church. The asymmetrical massing and central tower give Byram's house an Italianate character, but as the astronomer is said to have used the tower as an observatory, function probably outweighed fashion in the design of this unusual dwelling. (EF)

198. NATHAN TINKER HOUSE (NOW THE AMERICAN HOTEL)

Main Street, Sag Harbor (accessible to the public). The lower end of Main Street has been swept by fire four times, leaving little trace of the commercial waterfront it once was. After the blaze of 1845, when Sag Harbor's fortunes were at their zenith, cabinet-maker Nathan Tinker replaced the wooden shop he had lost with this handsome "fireproof structure," soon known as the "Tinker

Block." With its crenellated cornice, clustered storefront colonnettes, steep corner finial and drip-molded window lintels, this straightforward brick building is ornamented in the Gothic Revival style. In 1876 it was converted from residences (which probably had ground-floor stores) to the hotel it remains today. The wooden porch was added during the renovation. (EF)

198

199

199. THE CUSTOM HOUSE

Main and Garden Streets, Sag Harbor (museum — open to the public: 941-9444). The designation of Sag Harbor as a United States Customs Port of Entry in 1789 reveals the extent of maritime trade that flourished here. The busy harbor that was, in 1845, home to 63 whaling ships now shelters pleasure crafts in the summer season. It was in this five-bay Federal house that the first custom master, Henry Packer Dering, collected duties on whale oil, whalebone and other imported goods, and decided which spirits were potent enough to bear the label "Jamaican proof." The symmetrical window placement, with nine-over-nine sash and the delicate tracery in the transom over the entry, are all hallmarks of the somewhat austere Federal style. Built ca. 1795, the Custom House was home to three generations of Derings who witnessed the beginnings of the whaling industry that shaped Sag Harbor and watched the last whaler leave the harbor in 1871. Owned by the Society for the Preservation of Long Island Antiquities since 1966, the building has been restored to represent the years during which Dering was custom master, and is operated as a house museum furnished with a number of Dering family pieces. (KB)

200. SYBIL DOUGLAS HOUSE

Main Street, Sag Harbor (private residence — not open to the public). Built in the 1790s by the first of three seafaring Benjamin Hunttings, the house originally stood south of Garden Street, where the Whaling Museum is today. With its gambrel roof, modillioned cornice, elliptical-windowed facade gable, symmetrical plan and dramatic doorway, this house assimilates some details of the robust Late Georgian in the overall delicacy of its appearance. Huntting was the shipbuilder and owner who sent the first successful deep-sea whaler, the *Lucy*, out of Sag Harbor in 1785. When the second Benjamin Huntting decided to build a more fashionable mansion, he sold this house to a Captain Douglas, who moved it to this site in 1838. The side and rear wings were added in 1840. (EF)

201. HANNIBAL FRENCH HOUSE

Main Street, Sag Harbor (private residence — not open to the public). Hannibal & Stephen French was one of the last great Sag Harbor seafaring firms, one that made the transition from sail to steam and thus continued profitably after the whaling boom was over. With its spiral-twisted porch columns, bracketed cornice with fleurs-de-lis (a visual reference to the owner's name) and heavy-pedimented window lintels, this Italianate villa suggests the richness and elaboration of taste that often closes periods of prosperity and classicism. Tradition has it that Hannibal French commissioned Minard Lafever, designer of the Whaler's Church and of Benjamin Huntting's house next door on Main Street, to orchestrate the renovations of ca. 1860 to this early-nineteenth-century house, purchased from the Howell family. Whether the work of Lafever or of someone else, the French house reveals a sure and gifted hand in the rich impact of its Renaissance detail. (EF)

200

201

202. HOPE HOUSE

Main Street, Sag Harbor (private residence — not open to the public). Jeweler F. B. Hope built this mansard-roofed Second Empire house ca. 1865, when most Sag Harbor families were making do with older dwellings built when the economy was better. Three bays wide, with its entrance on one side and an ell beside the main block, this house is essentially similar to its Greek Revival neighbors, except for its ornamental detail. The high, slate-covered roof allows a full-height third floor (an improvement over the slant-walled top-floor rooms built a decade earlier), and the brackets paired below the heavy cornice indicate a post–Civil War construction date. Houses like this one were common elsewhere on Long Island in the 1870s, in places that grew as industry thrived nearby. The rarity of this kind of house in Sag Harbor is mute evidence to the backwater quiet that washed over the town in its somnolent period before the artists and the summer people wakened it to a new life. (EF)

202

203

203. JOHN JERMAIN MEMORIAL LIBRARY

Main Street, Sag Harbor (accessible to the public). The Neo-classic Revival brick-and-marble John Jermain Library, built in 1910 to the designs of New York architect Augustus N. Allen, is an anchor on Sag Harbor's Main Street. Its monumental fluted Doric columns support a broad pediment crowned by anthemion acroteria, and a deep triglyph-and-metope entablature encircles the building above the second story. Shallow brick antae articulate the side walls, framing the window bays. The building is crowned by a dome that rises 60 feet from the ground. The library was given to Sag Harbor by Mrs. Russell Sage, philanthropist and widow of Russell Sage, in memory of her father, Major John Jermain. (EF)

204. PELEG LATHAM HOUSE

Main Street, north of Madison Street, Sag Harbor (accessible to the public). This tall, center-chimneyed Federal-style house of ca. 1790 stood on Sag Harbor's main route to the waterfront near a bustling cluster of warehouses, chandleries, bakeries and other maritime businesses during the town's seaport era. It nestles into a slope that is the remnant of Turkey Hill, which rose from the harbor before the town scooped its heights to fill swamps and grade streets. Designed with a residence above and a commercial story at street level, the Peleg Latham house is a typical Sag Harbor merchant's house. (EF)

205. L'HOMMEDIEU HOUSE

Main Street, Sag Harbor (private residence — not open to the public). The brick town house of ca. 1840, which would be as much at home in Greenwich Village as in Sag Harbor, was built for Samuel L'Hommedieu, the great-grandson of a Huguenot fugitive from France. Every detail is simple and restrained; the building is quietly elegant. The wood door surround, with its pair of fluted Doric columns *in antis* screening the sidelighted door, is unique in Sag Harbor, where brick buildings of this period are rare. The L'Hommedieu family, pre-Revolutionary residents of Sag Harbor, operated a rope walk on Glover Street, in which they spun cables and lines for the rigging of local ships. (EF)

Sag Harbor

206

206. MUNICIPAL BUILDING

Main Street, Sag Harbor (accessible to the public). The three-story brick Municipal Building, originally the Mansion House Hotel, was built at the same time as the Tinker House (now the American Hotel) [*see* No. 198]. In 1873, while Sag Harbor was sinking into its post-whaling days of decline, the Mansion House became a school. The building's brownstone window lintels and the clustered colonnettes at its ground-floor front are like those at the American Hotel. Its deep, double-bracketed Italianate cornice and cupola date from the 1870s renovation. (EF)

207. OLD WHALER'S CHURCH (FIRST PRESBYTERIAN CHURCH OF SAG HARBOR)

Union Street, Sag Harbor (accessible to the public). In 1843–44, at the golden peak of the whaling age, a group of maritime magnates determined to rebuild the Presbyterian church to reflect their prosperity. The massive, tripartite facade, reminiscent of ancient Egyptian temple pylons, with corners sloped solidly to the ground, was designed by the talented New York architect Minard Lafever. One of the major monuments of the Egyptian Revival style in America, the church exhibits ornament that is unmistakably Sag Harbor seafaring, the deep cornice being topped by a handsome cresting of blubber spades. Perfect as its composition seems today, the church originally had a tall, telescoping tower that was a landmark from far offshore. An exotic stylistic confection of Chinese, Greek and English Renaissance echoes, the steeple blew down in the famous hurricane of September 1938. (EF) *207A: A view of the steeple.*

208. BENJAMIN HUNTTING HOUSE
(NOW THE SAG HARBOR WHALING MUSEUM AND HISTORICAL SOCIETY)

Main Street, corner of Garden Street, Sag Harbor (museum — accessible to the public). Like the Old Whaler's Church [*see* No. 207] also attributed to Minard Lafever, this boldly designed merchant's mansion of ca. 1845 is a tribute to the industry that brought a quarter-century of opulence to this town. It is Long Island's finest example of high-style Greek Revival architecture. Like the first Benjamin Huntting, whose house stood on this site (Sybil Douglas house, later farther north on Main Street [*see* No. 200], the owner of this mansion made his fortune in whaling ships. The airy crest surmounting the cornice proclaims the trade — it alternates the shapes of flensing knives and blubber spades around the roof. The ground floor houses the Sag Harbor Whaling Museum, a rich and varied collection of Sag Harbor's own souvenirs of its potent past. Few local history museums are as successful as this one in conveying the spirit of a place to their visitors. (EF) *208A: The stair well.*

208

209. STANTON HOUSE

Main and Madison Streets, Sag Harbor (private residence — not open to the public). This house was built for the son of Captain David Hand, said to be James Fenimore Cooper's model for Natty Bumppo of the Leatherstocking Tales. (It was erected on the site of a tiny cottage originally built in the early 1700s in Southampton, that now stands, on its fourth site, on Church Street.) The Greek Revival Stanton House is typical of the handsome, solid houses built for families who prospered along with Sag Harbor in the 1840s. There are scores of these houses everywhere in the village: two stories tall, their gable-ends forming pediments along the streets, their elegant doorways a catalogue of local builders' skills. This one, with its eagle leaded triangular gable-field window, its dentilled cornices and patterned pilasters defining its corners, is a classic in Greek Revival domestic design. The front porch with its lacy, scroll-sawn "gingerbread" trim is a restoration of the porch that was added to the house in the 1870s. Admiral Oscar Stanton, who was a later resident of the house, accompanied Commodore Perry on the voyage to Japan in 1853 that resulted in the opening of the country's trade with the West. Coincidentally, Stanton's father was the talented craftsman who built this house for Captain Hand. (EF)

209

210. VAN SCOY HOUSE

Main Street, corner Jefferson Street, Sag Harbor (private residence — not open to the public). The deep gambrel roof, the bold cornice with stylized modillion blocks and the elaborate doorway of this house built in 1810 herald the work of Benjamin Glover, a Sag Harbor builder whose own house stands farther south on Main Street at the corner of Glover Street. The gambrel end of the house, which fronts on an angled corner, is a masterly composition of windows and wall, roof slope and chimneys. Arnold Van Scoy, the mid-nineteenth-century resident, was a daguerreotype photographer whose pictures capture the world of the 1850s so that we can glimpse it and imagine it today. (EF)

210

211

211. JARED WADE HOUSE

Union Street, corner Madison Street, Sag Harbor (private residence — not open to the public). The unusual Federal-style doorway of this 1797 house is one of the most distinctive architectural features found in Sag Harbor. The delicately elaborate "mantel-frame" door surround encloses a leaded transom and sidelight windows in the traditional style. But above the cornice, a semielliptical fanlight (needed to light an upper space) adds a surprisingly satisfying graceful note to the composition. The house, built for a Captain Winters, is named for a later owner. Jared Wade was a whaling-era shipbuilder and captain whose swift *Montevideo* sped Sag Harbor gold seekers to California in 1849. (EF)

212. CAROLINE CHURCH OF BROOKHAVEN

Dyke Road, Setauket (accessible to the public). Erected in 1729, the Caroline Church is now the oldest Episcopal edifice on Long Island. Upon its consecration, it was named for George II's queen, who sent a silver communion service and altar cloths. While the church weathered the Revolutionary War under the protection of occupying British troops, the years that followed were hard for the congregation, as many Anglican Loyalists fled to Canada and England. By 1878, however, prosperity was sufficient for substantial interior redecoration, which occurred again in 1886. The present stained glass was added during these changes, as was the north wing parish hall. The tower, twisted with age, was substantially strengthened in 1986. The parish office and school, formerly the rectory, dates from about 1875, but was enlarged in 1967. The present interior appearance dates from 1937, when parishioner Ward Melville and his architect, Richard Haviland Smythe, installed the altar paneling, rails and wooden barrel vault. (NL)

213. SATTERLY–JERGENSON HOUSE

Old Field Road, Setauket (private residence — not open to the public). William Satterly of Setauket drowned ca. 1678 on a return voyage from Milford, Connecticut, where he had taken grain to be milled. Ironically, his descendant, Colonel Isaac Satterly, who served with distinction in the War of 1812, owned a gristmill near Setauket. Colonel Isaac is said to have lived his entire life (1765–1859) in this house, but it is thought to have been built earlier than the mid eighteenth century as it retains such seventeenth-century or First Period features as a boldly turned staircase and a casement window. Located just west of Setauket Mill Pond, the two-story, three-bay "half-house" is of a common Long Island house type. "Half-house" refers to the asymmetrical arrangement of the three bays, which appear to be half of a five-bay, center-hall house type. The house was completely restored in 1969 by Ward Melville, a philanthropist active in preserving early buildings in the region. (KB)

212

213

Setauket

159

FIRST PERIOD ARCHITECTURE

A

B

*L*ong Island's First Period structures, those dating from the seventeenth and early eighteenth centuries, are widely scattered among the original villages and rural enclaves of Nassau and Suffolk counties. Many are administered as house museums, while others survive as the earliest sections of houses that have been enlarged over time. Only the Massachusetts Bay Colony (Salem, Ipswich, etc.) now preserves a greater concentration of First Period structures, and efforts are under way to document and preserve this little-known aspect of Long Island's architectural heritage.

Unlike the predominantly Dutch settlements of western Long Island (present-day Kings, Queens and Nassau counties), the English communities of Suffolk County were settled for the most part by splinter groups originating from Massachusetts and Rhode Island. A characteristic one- or two-story house form, with center and flanking principal rooms, was transplanted here from New England by these settlers. The "Old House" in Cutchogue (1649) preserves the restored narrow oak clapboards,

A: Thompson House (ca. 1700), Setauket. B: Summer beam, parlor, Thompson House. C: Mulford House (1680), East Hampton. D: The "Old House" (1649), Cutchogue. E: Cross sections showing framing and chimney, the "Old House."

160

C

leaded casement windows and clustered medieval brick chimney associated with the period. A later generation continued to build in this tradition: The Mulford House in East Hampton (1680), for example, was of two full stories before it received a lean-to against the back wall in the early eighteenth century. Unique on Long Island, however, were its pair of facade gables that linked the structure stylistically to such landmarks as the Ironworks House in Saugus (1680) and the celebrated House of the Seven Gables in Salem (1668).

Common to many of Long Island's First Period structures is the summer beam, a colossal framing element exposed at the ceiling level, that serves to tie the outside wall to the inner frame and support the floor joists of the upper story. Often treated with decorative chamfers at the edges, this archaic timber disappeared toward the end of the period as houses of comparatively lighter construction became popular. Simultaneously, the integral lean-to form or "saltbox" house, with its back kitchen and ancillary rooms protected beneath a long sloping roofline, replaced the earlier two-story type. Examples of transitional houses, such as the Thompson House (ca. 1700) in Setauket, preserve both summer beam and integral lean-to, and are evidence of the evolution of house construction in the early eighteenth century. Simultaneously, the use of wood shingles on both roof and walls replaced the earlier tradition of clapboards, and the introduction of wooden sash windows in place of the medieval leaded casements signaled the end of the First Period on Long Island. (ZS)

D

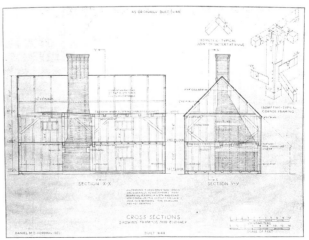

E

161

214

215

Setauket

162

214. SETAUKET POST OFFICE

Main Street and Mill Pond, Setauket (open to the public). A Greek Revival revival, the little temple-front Setauket village post office was built in 1941 to complement the historic town center and the adjacent Frank Melville Memorial Park established at the Lower Mill Pond in 1937. The four delicately proportioned columns supporting the portico were copied by the building's architect Richard Haviland Smythe from the corn-stalk-order columns designed by Benjamin Latrobe for the United States Capitol in 1808. The post office, on the north side of Main Street, replaces the previous post office, which occupied a house on the same site. Prior to 1925, Setauket's post office shared space in a store, now demolished, that stood across the street. (EF)

215. SETAUKET PRESBYTERIAN CHURCH

Caroline Avenue, Setauket. The present Setauket Presbyterian Church is the third to serve this congregation, which was organized about 1660. The first, built in 1674, was replaced in 1714 by a meeting house which was very nearly destroyed when used as a fort by occupying British forces between 1775 and 1783. When it was destroyed by a lightning strike, Sam Satterly and Clark Tooker were asked to erect the present church, dedicated in 1812. The simplicity of this Federal-period traditional design is marked by fine proportions and subtle decoration confined to the tower, entrance and interior-shuttered windows. Much original work has been preserved inside as well, despite some changes made in 1868. A Sunday School wing of that date was replaced in 1961 by the present wing. (NL)

216. THE MANOR OF ST. GEORGE, SELAH B. STRONG HOUSE

116 Dyke Road, Strong's Neck, Setauket (private residence — not open to the public). Strong's Neck was purchased by Col. William Smith on October 22, 1686 and was constituted with later purchases as the Manor of St. George by patents of 1693 and 1697. Called "Tangier" Smith to distinguish him from other members of the Smith family (he had served as Governor of Tangier, Morocco), Col. Smith erected the first of three manor houses on this site overlooking Conscience Bay. During the Revolutionary War the property was owned by Selah Strong, who had married the great-granddaughter of "Tangier" Smith in 1760 and was the builder of the second manor house. His wife, Anna Smith Strong, from her vantage point at the manor, was a vital communications link between the Setauket spy ring and Washington's headquarters in Connecticut during the British occupation of Long Island. The present house was erected in 1845 by Judge Selah B. Strong on the site of the two earlier manor houses. Designed by the prominent English-born architect Frederick Diaper (1810–1906), who had married a cousin of Judge Strong, the restrained Greek Revival house with Italianate influences is characterized by transverse gables on each of its four sides and a porticoed entrance door. (CT)

216

217

218

217. THOMPSON HOUSE

North Country Road, Setauket (open to the public: 941-9444). The Thompson House (ca. 1700) is one of Setauket's oldest surviving dwellings. Dr. Samuel Thompson, a practicing physician and Revolutionary War captain, is credited with the addition to the main house that contained the doctor's library and medical office. His son, Benjamin F. Thompson, was born in the house and later became famous as Long Island's first great historian. A lawyer by profession, the younger Thompson authored his *History of Long Island* in 1839. The house is of the integral lean-to type — i.e., its back extension, containing the kitchen and small end rooms on the first floor and an unfinished loft above, was built contemporaneously with the larger two-story main block. Origi-

nal oak clapboards survive beneath the oversized shingles of the north facade, and other early features include chamfered summer beams and corner posts that are hallmarks of its First Period construction date. The house was acquired by Ward Melville in 1946 and restored by Port Jefferson architect Daniel Perry between 1946 and 1950. Owned by the Stony Brook Community Fund and leased by the Society for the Preservation of Long Island Antiquities since 1951, the Thompson House is open to the public from June to mid-October and houses one of the finest collections of seventeenth- and eighteenth-century furniture on Long Island. (ZS)

218. MALTBY PAYNE HOUSE

105 North Ferry Road, Shelter Island (private residence — not open to the public). The Greek Revival, mirroring in architecture the young nation's embrace of the democratic ideals of ancient Greece, is spoken of as the first American architectural style because it was popular not only in cities, but also — in its vernacular form — in the small towns and villages of America. Gabriel Crook, an architect-builder native to Shelter Island, de-

signed and built the Maltby Payne House ca. 1840. A representative example of Crook's vernacular Greek Revival work that retains its exterior integrity, the Payne House stands one-and-a-half stories tall and three bays wide, with a side hall entrance typical of its period. Fluted pilasters, Doric columns supporting the porch and dentils at the cornice are all hallmarks of the vernacular Greek Revival style. (KB)

219. "SYLVESTER MANOR"

80 North Ferry Road, Shelter Island (private residence — not open to the public). Nathaniel Sylvester, a wealthy English shipping merchant, purchased Shelter Island in 1652 for 1600 pounds of sugar. Despite experiencing a shipwreck on their voyage from England, Sylvester and his new bride were able to build the first manor that same year. The manor was largely destroyed by fire, but elements of it were incorporated into the present manor,

built in 1733 by Nathaniel's grandson and last Lord of the Manor, Brinley Sylvester. The hip roof, pedimented gable-roof dormers, two-story pilasters and paired interior chimneys bespeak the Georgian style. The privy, with hip roof, interior wood paneling and a pair of windows flanking the door, is an elegant reflection of the manor house. "Sylvester Manor" is noted as the site of one of the few identified slave burial grounds on Long Island. (KB)

220

220. HISTORIC BUILDINGS AT BLYDENBURGH COUNTY PARK

New Mill Road, Smithtown (open to the public: 360-4966).
This 560-acre county park lies in the Nissequoque River basin between Hauppauge and Jericho Turnpike. At its center is the remains of the last and largest milling complex built in Smithtown, begun in 1798 by Joshua and Caleb Smith II, cousins, and another relative, Isaac Blydenburgh, all of whom held land in the valley. They built an earthen dam and a sawmill, and in 1827 a fulling mill was established for the processing of woolen cloth in the former Presbyterian Church building that had been relocated from the Village of the Branch. The site also included a tannery and shoe factory, a public landing and a store. After years of decline, the gristmill closed in 1924. Surviving buildings in the county park, created in 1965, include the two-story gristmill powered by two horizontal or turbine wheels (being restored), the gambrel-roofed miller's house of 1802 with an unusual two-story porch (seen here), the second Blydenburgh house (1821) and a small cottage in the Gothic Style (ca. 1850), one of the few in Suffolk County. (NL)

221. CALEB SMITH II HOUSE (NOW SMITHTOWN HISTORICAL SOCIETY)

North Country Road, Smithtown (open to the public: 265-6768). Probably the finest Federal house in Smithtown, this structure was originally erected in Commack and moved to the center of Smithtown in 1955. The house was built by Caleb Smith II (1736–1831), who in 1819 gave his house in Hauppauge to his daughter Sarah as a wedding present and moved to Commack to build a new house for himself. Smith actually enlarged a small seventeenth-century dwelling already on the site, now the south or right-hand side of the present structure. He added the wide center hall and four rooms on the north side and the four end chimneys, and updated all the interior woodwork which, based on stylistic evidence, was probably the work of George Curtis, builder of the 1825 Presbyterian Church [*see* No. 223]. The house descended in the Smith and Burr families until 1955 when, threatened by demolition, it was moved to its present site to serve as the headquarters of the Smithtown Historical Society, founded that same year. (NL)

222. "THE HOMESTEAD," JUDGE J. LAWRENCE SMITH HOUSE

205 Middle Country Road, Village of the Branch Historic District, Smithtown (under restoration). The Historic District of the Village of the Branch consists of ten two-and-a-half-story white shingle houses, most of which were built between 1720 and 1830, and represents the most important surviving historic district of its type between New York City and Riverhead. A pivotal structure in the District is "The Homestead," the home of Judge J. Lawrence Smith (1816–1889). A lawyer and surrogate judge of Suffolk County for almost 40 years, Judge Smith was active in local politics, wrote a history of Smithtown in 1882 and maintained his estate as a working farm. The core of the house was built in the eighteenth century by the descendants of Richard Blydenburgh and it passed to the Judge in 1845. When "The Homestead" passed to Smith's son, James Clinch Smith, some exterior modifications were undertaken in 1897 by Stanford White, who had married Clinch's youngest sister. White's changes include the dormers and center gable with a fanlight and a full-length front porch with 17 Doric columns, since removed. Also part of the district is the Epenetus Smith Tavern (211 Middle Country Road), which functioned as the social and political center of Smithtown from 1750 into the early years of the nineteenth century. Both structures are owned by the Smithtown Historical Society. (NL)

221

222

Smithtown

167

223. SMITHTOWN PRESBYTERIAN CHURCH

Middle Country Road and River Road, Smithtown (accessible to the public). Erected between 1823 and 1825 by local builder and woodcarver George Curtis, who also executed the fine woodwork of the interior, the Smithtown Presbyterian Church was dedicated in 1827. Constructed at a cost of $2100, the church replaced an earlier small frame meetinghouse that was moved from Smithtown's first settlement site about four miles north in 1750. The design is similar to Federal churches built in Huntington in 1784 and Setauket in 1812. While smaller than these, the Smithtown Presbyterian Church displays more architectural detail. The pilasters, full pediment and engaged tower with its unusual design made it an impressive contribution to Smithtown in 1825. The original box pews, high pulpit and clear-glass windows have never been altered. The balcony carries a later organ at the north end. In 1892 a social hall was added at the back and a series of modern additions were begun in 1963, housing offices and Sunday school rooms. (NL)

224. "THE ORCHARD," JAMES L. BREESE ESTATE (NOW WHITEFIELD CONDOMINIUMS)

Hill Street, Southampton (private residences — not open to the public; can be seen from the road). A significant landmark in the village of Southampton, and one of the early large summer residences, or "cottages," to be built in the village, the Colonial Revival–style Breese mansion has recently been sympathetically readapted for condominiums. Construction of the house evolved from 1897 to 1906, under the supervision of the nationally known architectural firm of McKim, Mead & White. Built for James L. Breese, New York financier and close friend of both Charles McKim and Stanford White, "The Orchard" is a prominent example of a special architectural trend — the rediscovery of an "American" building tradition and an attempt to recreate the "colonial" style on a modern scale. McKim, Mead & White were instrumental in popularizing the Colonial Revival style during the late nineteenth century, and the Breese estate, with its Mount Vernon–inspired portico, actually incorporates an existing nineteenth-century farmhouse in its core. The central section of the house is flanked by two wings, the east wing containing the music room. Designed by Stanford White ca. 1906 and measuring 70′ × 28′, its interior walls are lined with linenfold paneling. (CT)

225

225. CANOE PLACE INN

Canoe Place Road and Bathing Beach Road, Southampton (open to the public). If a building can be "invested with style," William Lawrence Bottomley (1883–1951), the accomplished country-house architect once noted, "that intangible quality, that stamp, which gives it life and individuality will be both sound and original." Bottomley's reconstruction of the ancient Canoe Place Inn at Hampton Bays after it was largely destroyed by fire on July 4, 1921 had all of those qualities. While following the original lines, Bottomley employed a variety of roof and dormer shapes that juxtaposed to break up the linear appearance of the exterior while unifying the sprawling complex with a sweeping second-floor veranda.

The charming Colonial Revival watering spot was considered the "cat's meow" in the Roaring Twenties as hundreds flocked to its Saturday-night dances. Governor Al Smith made it his summer home for many years (there were cottages on the grounds) and its illustrious list of visitors included F.D.R., John L. Sullivan, Helen Hayes, Albert Einstein, Cary Grant and such local notables as Waxey Gordon, one of the East End's leading bootleggers. While the inn's postwar history has been somewhat checkered, it remains a building worth preserving. Bottomley went on to design 11 country houses on Long Island, including his own in Brookville. Among the best-known commissions of the École des Beaux-Arts–trained architect, who was awarded the McKim fellowship at the American Academy in Rome, is Manhattan's River House (1932). (RBM) *225A: The inn and cottages in an old postcard view.*

225A

226

227

226. WILLIAM MERRITT CHASE HOUSE

Canoe Place and Bathing Beach Road, Shinnecock Hills, Southampton (private residence — not open to the public). Lured to Southampton by the gift of land on a bluff, the prominent New York and Brooklyn painter William Merritt Chase decided to establish a summer home and an art "school on the sands" in 1891. He asked McKim, Mead & White to build his house and studio (done gratis for a fellow artist), and by the summer of 1892 he was in residence, leading an art colony a few miles away. From the sober, dignified Shingle Style house with its deep gambrel roof punctuated by dormers, Chase ventured onto the dunes and to the water's edge to catch the lights and shades of the South Shore. Chase closed his art colony after 1902, continuing to use his house, which still stands, into the teens. (EF)

227. "HOLLYHOCKS," HALSEY HOUSE

South Main Street, Southampton (museum — open to the public: 283-2494). The Thomas Halsey House is dated ca. 1648 by some scholars, making it the earliest house standing in Southampton. Halsey was a native of England who landed at Lynn, Massachusetts, and joined a party of settlers who founded Southampton in 1640. The house is a three-bay, two-story saltbox whose massive center chimney is characteristic of the First Period house type. The lean-to was an early addition, and a rear one-story extension was built in 1900, when the house was modernized. Purchased in 1927 by Henry Francis du Pont, founder of the Winterthur Museum, the house was restored and opened as a house museum in cooperation with the Southampton Colonial Society. Interpretation of the interior rooms is reflected by the front facade. The northern section of the house to the right of the center entry is believed to be the oldest portion, a one-room dwelling with chamber above, and is restored with seventeenth-century-type casement windows. The southern section to the left of the entry is believed to date no later than 1652, but has been installed as an eighteenth-century parlor and chamber reflecting the later occupants of the house, and six-over-six sash is employed in this area. The Thomas Halsey House is owned and administered by the Southampton Colonial Society. (KB)

228. PARRISH ART MUSEUM

25 Jobs Lane, Southampton (open to the public: 283-2118). Grosvenor Atterbury, later acclaimed for innovative low-cost housing at Forest Hills Gardens in Queens (begun 1909), designed this rambling one-story art museum for Samuel L. Parrish in 1898. The 29-year-old architect grew up familiar with the Southampton area, his father having been a pioneering colonist at Shinnecock Hills. The warm-colored, arcade-fronted brick museum sits behind a brick-and-iron fence in a garden ornamented with pedestaled busts of 18 Roman emperors. The museum, in its original building and a large fireproof hall added in 1903, holds a fine collection featuring Italian paintings and sculpture. (EF)

229

230

229. THE ROGERS MEMORIAL LIBRARY

9 Jobs Lane, Southampton (open to the public). Built in 1895 on the site of the Old Southampton Academy, the Library was established by Harriet Jones Rogers as a memorial to her mother. Plans for the Late Queen Anne–style building were donated by Robert H. Robertson, a New York architect who had worked for a time in the offices of George B. Post and William A. Potter.

A classic example of its period and style, the picturesquely massed library combines a brick ground floor with a stucco-and-half-timber upper story, while a polygonal corner turret with conical cap and a facade gable with deep vergeboards give the building an asymmetrical plan and irregular roofline. (EF)

230. SHINNECOCK HILLS GOLF CLUB

North Highway, Southampton (private club—not open to the public). Created with the help of Indians from the nearby reservation, Shinnecock Hills Golf Club (1891–92) was the first professionally designed course in America to be built in conjunction with a clubhouse. Willie Dunn, a prominent Scottish golfer, laid out the links over grass-covered dunes not unlike the moors of his native land, while McKim, Mead & White designed the shingle-clad clubhouse for a sport with which they were totally unfamiliar. Given an air of formality by the Doric porch columns and Palladian windows that encircled the building, the clubhouse was dramatically sited on a rise with panoramic views of hills, bay and ocean. Its founders, Edward S. Mead and Samuel Parrish [*see* Parrish Art Museum, No. 228], who formed the association that acquired the 80-acre site from the Long Island Improvement Company, were to watch the new sport flourish in the 1890s as the Shinnecock players, who wore red woolen coats, swept the first four USGA Women's Amateur Championships and, in 1896, played host to the second U.S. Open, held back-to-back on the 18-hole course with the U.S. Amateur Championship. (RBM)

231. SOUTHAMPTON HIGH SCHOOL (NOW SOUTHAMPTON TOWN HALL)

Hampton Road, Southampton. The former Southampton High School, considered when it was built in 1912 to be among the better examples of classical architecture in New York State, was one of the first important works by noted architect William Lawrence Bottomley (1883–1951). Bottomley, who began practicing in New York in 1911, was to become prominent as a designer of country estates under the firm name of Hewitt & Bottomley. After having won a national contest for the high-school project (which had stipulated that all the drawings be Colonial in style to blend in with the existing architecture of the town), Bottomley produced a classically symmetrical Georgian design highlighting quite early in his career his superb sense of scale and form. The exterior, clad in Colonial red brick with white marble trim, has a center three-story axial bay that projects several feet from the adjoining two-story wings. The tall Ionic-columned portico, with Palladian windows at the second story, lends added dramatic emphasis to the entrance, as does the pyramidal roof crowned by a graceful cupola. Bottomley's attention to elements of Georgian detail include the string-course at the level of the second-floor windows and the delicately carved swags and wreaths in the front pediment. The floor plan, in the shape of a cross, contained ten grade rooms, large study halls, recreation rooms and laboratories. While designing in a variety of eclectic styles, Bottomley was an admirer of the Georgian, publishing a two-volume book, *Great Georgian Houses of America*. His Southampton High School demonstrates his grasp of the elements of the style and his ability to compose them into a harmonious and impressive structure. Having remained vacant for a number of years, the former school has now been sympathetically renovated into a town hall. (CT)

232

233

Southampton
174

234

232 & 233. LUCIEN N. TYNG HOUSE AND PLAYHOUSE

Halsey Neck Lane, Southampton (private residence — not open to the public). Built in 1931, the Lucien Tyng house is one of the earliest examples of the International Style in America. Designed by Peabody, Wilson & Brown to replace an older residence on the site, the asymmetrical stucco building is a blocky composition of angular elements punctuated by crisply punched windows, many of which open two sides of a corner. The rambling two-story mass is anchored by a cluster of taller blocks that rise behind the entrance porch to enliven the straight roofline. Utilities executive Lucien Tyng and both his first and his second wives were patrons of the arts in Southampton, their commitment demonstrated by the handsome studio-theater they built (also designed by Peabody, Wilson & Brown, and completed in 1931) north and east of the main house. The deep cream colored stucco complex, interestingly roofed with crab-orchard sandstone tiles in pink, yellow and brown, featured a large auditorium in which plays and concerts were staged. Eleanor Brown, interior designer and wife of the studio's architect Archibald Brown, converted the playhouse into a weekend house in 1942. (EF)

234. CLEVELAND–CHARNEWS HOUSE

Main Road, Southold (private residence — not open to the public). The Cleveland–Charnews House has the distinction of being one of the earliest architect-designed buildings on Long Island. William D. Cochran, an architect-builder, designed, built and renovated several buildings in the area while working on the First Universalist Church of Southold [see No. 235] between 1835 and 1837. His assistant, Richard Lathers, later joined the distinguished architectural firm of Town and Davis. The unusual features that mark professional architectural influence are the segmental-arched dormers, which were not likely to have been found in the pattern books used by carpenters of the day. Cochran used the same dormer design on the nearby Hempstead–Hartranft House, which was, sadly, demolished in 1986. Architectural detail is limited to small brackets under the eaves on the main block and the west wing cornice. A short row of brackets adorns the cornice above the door, which is elaborated with sidelights containing tracery. (KB)

235

235. FIRST UNIVERSALIST CHURCH

Main Road, Southold (accessible to the public). A unique hybrid of the Greek Revival and Gothic styles, the First Universalist Church dominates the sweeping curve of Southold's Main Road. Built between 1835 and 1837 by William D. Cochran in association with Richard Lathers, artist, architect and landscape designer, First Universalist boasts perhaps the only Gothic Palladian window on Long Island. Cochran's attempt to fuse the two styles resulted in a surprisingly charming structure. Greek Revival features include the Doric corner pilasters and entrance front, while the pointed arched windows and battlemented tower, with its tall octagonal belfry crowned with spirelets and delicate window tracery, herald the Gothic influence. (CT) *235A: Architect's drawing.*

236. SOUTHOLD FREE LIBRARY

Main Street, Southold (accessible to the public). Built in 1891 to house the Southold Savings Bank, the red-brick and terra-cotta Romanesque Southold Free Library was designed by a local architect who was not averse to experimenting successfully in a variety of styles. George H. Skidmore of Riverhead was responsible for numerous country residences and business and public structures on eastern Long Island, including the Queen Anne/Shingle Style First Congregational Church in Riverhead (1909) and the impressive Riverhead Savings Bank Building (1892). His design for the Southold Savings Bank, a compact one-story build-ing with a parapet gable terminating in square brick posts, was an innovative addition to the Southold streetscape. Decorative elements on the otherwise plain structure include handsome iron window grates, granite coping and projecting brick headers in the upper half of the facade. In 1927 the bank moved into new quarters and Edna Cahoon Booth bought the property as a memorial to her parents, Mr. and Mrs. Edward Cahoon, country estate owners in Southold since 1900, and presented it to the Southold Free Library. (CT)

237. MILLS POND HOUSE

North Country Road, St. James (open to the public: 862-6575). The Mills Pond House in St. James, designed by the noted New York City architect Calvin Pollard in 1837, was completed by 1840. High-style front and back stoops boast fluted Doric columns; interior detailing, such as the Belgian marble chimneypieces and elaborate plaster ceiling medallions, are all characteristic of the Greek Revival mode. The original owners, William Wickham and Eliza Ann Mills, were descended from Timothy Mills, who came to Smithtown from Jamaica (Queens) in the early eighteenth century. Nine children were born to William Wickham Mills and his wife, evidently prompting this wealthy farmer and investor to replace their smaller dwelling which then occupied the site. The house passed through successive generations of the Mills–Smith family until its gift to the Town of Smithtown in 1976. It now serves as headquarters for the Smithtown Township Arts Council. (ZS)

238. "LAND OF CLOVER," LATHROP BROWN ESTATE

Long Beach Road, St. James (private residence — not open to the public). "Land of Clover," built between 1915 and 1918 for Lathrop Brown (brother of Archibald Brown of Peabody, Wilson & Brown, who designed the estate buildings), is an ambitious Southern Georgian-style mansion reminiscent of "Westover" on Virginia's James River. The two-and-a-half-story main block, built of hand-molded brick with wood trim, is centered by a door surmounted by a massive broken-scroll pediment, and is con- nected to two end pavilions by curving hyphens. The estate's original outbuildings include a superintendent's cottage, five-car garage, barn complex, water tower and an elaborate, 22-stall horseshoe-shaped stable. The Brown estate demonstrates Pea- body, Wilson & Brown's facility for the Colonial Revival manner. At the time this complex was designed, Archibald Brown was living nearby in the remodeled "East Farm." (EF)

239. KNOX SCHOOL STABLES

Long Beach Road, St. James (Nissequoque) (private school — not open to the public). One of the more architec- turally interesting aspects of the country-house phenomenon on Long Island was the design consideration given in estate planning to outbuildings, both functionally and aesthetically. Within this category, the building that often received the most attention, both by architect and owner, was the stable complex or farm group. The horseshoe-shaped Knox School stable is an excellent example and may owe its unique plan to the "Panopticon," eighteenth-century philosopher Jeremy Bentham's influential circular prison design. The timber-frame shingled structure was built between 1914 and 1916 on the estate of Lathrop Brown, brother of Archibald Brown, the architect and partner in the prominent firm of Peabody, Wilson & Brown, who were the designers of the estate. The stable con- tained 22 box stalls facing a covered exercise track, with trainer's and groom's cottages at the open end of the horseshoe. Acquired by the Knox School in 1953, the stable is unaltered and was, until recently, used for its original purpose. (CT)

240. "DEEPWELLS"

North Country Road, St. James (not open to the public — undergoing renovation). "Deepwells," a large Greek Revival country house built for Joel L. G. Smith in 1847, is said to have been patterned after the Mills Pond House (1837), which is located nearby on North Country Road [*see* No. 237]. Smith (1819–1876) was descended from the "Bull" Smiths of Smithtown and was one of the founders of the St. James Episcopal Church [*see* No. 241], for which he donated the land in 1853. Smith sold "Deepwells" to Milton H. Smith of New York after the Civil War, and it was later acquired by William J. Gaynor, a famous "reform mayor" of the City of New York, who improved the property as a summer place and lived there until his death in 1913. The house has recently been acquired by Suffolk County and is undergoing restoration. "Deepwells" is architecturally distinguished as a large, imposing builder's house of the late Greek Revival period. It incorporates decorative wooden porch columns, a belvedere and other fine exterior detailing as well as elaborate plaster ornamenta- tion and marble mantelpieces in the principal rooms. Front and back parlor were converted into a large, single room by Mayor Gaynor by removing the parlor "screen." As a whole, however, the house remains essentially intact from the construction period. (ZS)

238

239

240

St. James

179

241. ST. JAMES EPISCOPAL CHURCH

North Country Road, St. James (accessible to the public). The northeastern quarter of Smithtown, historically known as Sherrowogue, took the name of St. James following the establishment of the St. James Episcopal Church in 1853. Completed to the plans of the leading ecclesiastical architect Richard Upjohn (1802–1878; designer of Trinity Church in Manhattan) and erected in 1854, the church is the earliest Gothic Revival structure in Smithtown. The steep roof and board-and-batten siding with Gothic pointed windows takes its inspiration from English rural parish churches, and is consistent with the Anglican roots of Episcopalianism. As built, the delicate porch over the front door stood against the sanctuary; in the 1870s the porch was moved forward and the present tower built to the designs of Upjohn or his son, Richard M. Upjohn. Its tracery decoration is noteworthy. Stanford White, whose country home "Box Hill" was nearby [*see* No. 245], was a parishioner here and designed three of the stained-glass memorial windows, executed by Tiffany Studios. The church remained unaltered until the addition of the parish hall wing in 1961. (NL)

242. ST. JAMES RAILROAD STATION

Lake and Railroad Avenues, St. James (open to the public). A charming reminder of an age when most of the Long Island Rail Road's depots and freight houses were board-and-batten buildings, the St. James Station has been sheltering passengers for more than a century. Its polychromatic color scheme, bracketed eaves and "gingerbread" trim were the work of Calvin L'Hommedieu, who erected the building in 1873. Inside, a large potbellied stove once warmed the unadorned waiting room. This photograph dates from the early 1950s. (RBM)

243

244

243. "TIMOTHY HOUSE"

North Country Road, St. James (private residence — not open to the public). "Timothy House," built ca. 1800 by a descendant of the founder of Smithtown, Richard "Bull" Smith, and named for later owner Timothy C. Smith, was bought ca. 1906 by architect and Smith descendant Lawrence Smith Butler. Butler added the west section of the house and the dormers and moved the structure back from its original site closer to the road. Typical of its period, "Timothy House" was originally constructed as a two-and-a-half-story "half house," with a wing and shed-roofed slave kitchen. An unusual feature is the wide-sweeping Dutch Colonial gambrel roof of the wing, its pitch matching that of the main house, and the only roof of its kind known to be in existence on Long Island. The section of the house dating from ca. 1800 retains its front stoop with slender octagonal posts, one of just a few surviving examples of this type of entrance. The 12 acres of farmland that form the setting for this house and the allée of sugar maples that line the driveway add to the atmosphere of this scenic section of Route 25A. (CT)

244. WETHERILL HOUSE

Moriches Road, St. James (private residence — not open to the public). Designed by Stanford White for Kate Smith Wetherill (widow of the Rev. Joseph B. Wetherill and sister of White's wife, Bessie Smith), the shingled three-story octagonal house was built in 1895. Dramatically sited at the crest of a hill overlooking Stony Brook Harbor, the Wetherill House is, as was White's own "Box Hill" [see No. 245], characterized by its use of dominating gables, but here each face of the octagon is surmounted by a gable with alternating round-headed and Palladian windows. Bessie's marriage to Stanford White sparked a flowering of country-house architecture in St. James among the Smith daughters. In addition to "Box Hill" and the Wetherill house, the firm of McKim, Mead & White was involved in the design of two other houses for Bessie's sisters — "By-the-Harbor" for Cornelia Smith (Mrs. Prescott Hall Butler) in 1878 and the enlargement of "Sherrewogue" for Ella B. Smith (Mrs. Devereau Emmet) in 1895. (CT)

245. "Box Hill," Stanford White Estate

Moriches Road, St. James (private residence — not open to the public). "Box Hill," the summer home of the talented and flamboyant architect Stanford White, is a rambling multigabled house. White, a partner in the nationally known firm of McKim, Mead & White, had married Bessie Springs Smith, youngest daughter of Judge J. Lawrence Smith of Smithtown, in 1884. Originally a simple, mid-nineteenth-century farmhouse, the structure was enlarged and remodeled by the architect on at least three occasions: 1886, 1892 and 1902. "Box Hill's" pebble-dashed stucco wall treatment and elaborate Neo-Colonial detail, including paired Ionic columns framing the entrance and delicately deco-

rated sidelights, are its most expressive exterior features. The eclectic interiors illustrate White's rejection of any single style and include walls covered with split bamboo, a staircase of green tile and sixteenth-century Italian spiral pillars. The beautifully landscaped grounds contained a *Diana* by Augustus Saint Gaudens, a reduced-size model of the one that crowned Madison Square Garden, White's favorite of all the buildings he designed. On the National Register of Historic Places and still in family hands today, "Box Hill" remains much as Stanford White created it. (CT) *245: The east facade. 245A: The west facade.*

245A

246. St. James Chapel
(now All Souls Episcopal Church)

Main Street, Stony Brook (accessible to the public). Stanford White, independently of his partners, designed this elegant little church in 1889 in Stony Brook, near his country seat. Before its completion, the congregation, established in 1857, met in a nearby school. The pointed tower, steep pitched roof and multiple-gabled dormers thrust the chapel skyward, while imposed buttresses root it in the ground. The sanctuary has a curved-truss ceiling painted with gold stars on a blue field and an 1885 tracker-action organ. The chapel's original bell, the gift of the first minister, still graces the tower belfry. (EF)

247. Hawkins–Mount Homestead

Route 25A and Stony Brook Road, Stony Brook (currently undergoing restoration). The Hawkins–Mount Homestead, now owned by the Stony Brook Community Fund and administered by the Museums at Stony Brook, is most notable for its historical association with the nineteenth-century genre painter William Sidney Mount (1807–1868). Major Eliazer Hawkins (1716–1791), the first known owner of the house, is credited with enlarging the eighteenth-century core of the dwelling to suit the needs of his wife and six children. A son, Major Jonas Hawkins, inherited the place and operated a store and tavern there as early as 1797. After his death in 1817, his widowed daughter Julia Ann Mount continued the business, providing a home for her talented children, one of whom was William Sidney Mount. The subject of many Mount paintings and sketches, the house underwent alterations in the Victorian period and was restored to its present appearance in the 1940s. (ZS)

Stony Brook

248

248. HEALTH SCIENCES CENTER, STATE UNIVERSITY OF NEW YORK AT STONY BROOK

Nicolls Road, Stony Brook (open to the public). Architect Bertrand Goldberg has called his imposing and futuristic Health Sciences Center at S.U.N.Y. Stony Brook a "megastructure." The huge three-tower complex, comprised of 1.2 million square feet (more than the Empire State Building), is one of the nation's newest and most sophisticated medical centers, containing five professional schools, laboratories, offices and a 540-bed hospital. The highest tower rises 324 feet — 19 stories — making it Long Island's tallest building and a well-known mariner's landmark. Goldberg was also the architect of the celebrated Marine Towers complex in Chicago. (RBM)

249. "PIN WHEEL" HOUSE

Watermill (private residence — not open to the public). One of the most experimental postwar houses to be built on Long Island — little more than a platform with a roof in the middle of a potato field — this 1954 house, designed for his own use by architect Peter Blake, used an ingenious system of sliding barn doors on tracks so that the house could be shut up easily during the winter months and reopened in summer. It set the tone for things to come in the way of small vacation homes. Blake, a curator of architecture and design at The Museum of Modern Art during the 1950s, was to originate a series of innovative vacation houses on eastern Long Island during this period. (AG)

249

250. TELEFUNKEN TRANSATLANTIC WIRELESS STATION

Cherry Avenue, west of Locust Avenue, West Sayville (not open to the public). In 1911, Kaiser Wilhelm of Germany sent the Telefunken Company, a group of engineers, to the United States to choose a site for a transatlantic wireless-communications station. In 1912 this powerful station was completed in West Sayville, on property bought by the German government. Another wireless station was constructed in Nauen, Germany, to communicate with Telefunken in America through spark-gap transmitters. On May 15, 1915, the *Lusitania* was struck after a coded message — "The *Lusitania* sailed past Sayville at 11 AM this morning" — was received at Nauen from West Sayville. The U.S. government immediately seized the property, and it is federally owned to the present day. Sayville resident Sewell Thornhill, Jr. is credited with decoding the message.

I. H. Green, a prominent architect from Sayville, designed the original powerhouse that stands on the property today. The Bason brothers, also of Sayville, built the project. Several outbuildings and huge concrete bases that stabilized the transatlantic communication antenna stand, in addition to the powerhouse, grouped near a modern Remote Communication Air to Ground (RCAG) tower. The RCAG tower is operated by the FAA and broadcasts to international air flights.

In addition to the historical importance of this 121-acre site and its significance to U.S. involvement in the First World War, the site supports the rare plant species Sandplain Gerardia (*Agalinis acuta*) and is one of ten places in the world where the wildflower grows. The property has recently won approval from a U.S. Senate/House Conference Committee for the creation of a 102-acre wildlife refuge, the Town of Islip being given recreational use of the remaining 19 acres. The fate of the powerhouse, however, remains unresolved. (KK) *250: The station. 250A: The RCAG tower.*

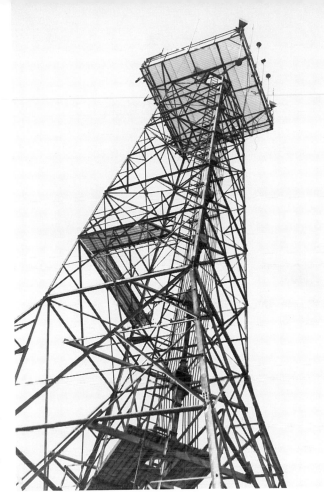

250A

250

West Sayville

185

251

251. HAWKINS–JACOBSEN HOUSE

Yaphank Avenue, Yaphank (museum, open to the public: 924-3401). Outwardly characteristic of a mid nineteenth-century Italianate or Tuscan-style country dwelling, the Hawkins–Jacobsen House appears to date from ca. 1870 and boasts such exterior detailing as heavily bracketed eaves, paired windows with prominent lintels, and a large cupola that surmounts its cross-axial roof plan. The house is an excellent and unspoiled example of the taste of a prosperous owner who in all probability selected the design from a contemporary builder's pattern book. Unlike many rural residences of central Long Island, however, the Hawkins–Jacobsen House employs decorative woodwork and a scale that sets it apart from the more restrained traditions of the region. Now owned by Suffolk County, the house is administered by the Yaphank Historical Society and is open to the public. (ZS)

252. ST. ANDREW'S EPISCOPAL CHURCH

Main Street, Yaphank (accessible to the public). The Gothic Revival style exerted a brief influence on Long Island in the 1850s and found a charming expression in St. Andrew's. Now documented as a virtual copy of Grace Church, Massapequa (1844, now altered), St. Andrew's was completed in 1854 on a plot of land given for the purpose by James H. Weeks. While preserving the simple rectangular form and plan of contemporary rural churches, St. Andrew's combines detailing such as roof crenelations, lancet windows and a battered front-door enframement that are hallmarks of vernacular Gothic Revival design. Introduction of the style may be credited to Weeks himself, a local resident and president of the Long Island Rail Road, who built his own house and a schoolhouse in the octagonal mode during this period. Weeks was related through marriage to William Sidney Smith, whose ancestral estate "Longwood" [see No. 194] was embellished in the Gothic Revival style at about this time. The church was declared a New York State Landmark in 1988. (ZS)

252

A

B

C

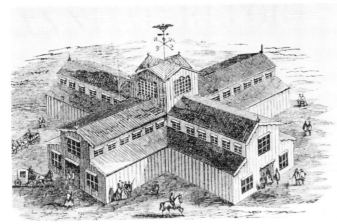

D

E

A: Joshua Brewster-Smith House, Hauppage; built in the late eighteenth century; demolished in the 1960s.
B: "Tryon Hall," Thomas Jones Residence, Massapequa; built 1770; demolished in the 1960s. C: Exhibition Hall of the Queens County Agricultural Society, Mineola; built 1841; demolished in the 1950s.
D: "Glenada," John Banvard Residence, Cold Spring Harbor; built 1852; demolished ca. 1900.
E: "Manhanset House," Shelter Island; built 1872; demolished 1910.

F

G

H

I

F: Garden City Hotel, by McKim, Mead & White, Garden City; built 1900; demolished in the 1970s. G: "Harbor Hill," Clarence Mackay Estate, by McKim, Mead & White, Roslyn; built 1900–02; demolished 1947. H: "Laurelton Hall," Louis Comfort Tiffany Estate, Cold Spring Harbor; built 1904; demolished 1957. I: Pinelawn Cemetery Railroad Station; built 1904; demolished ca. 1940s.

J

K

L

J: Château des Beaux Arts, by Delano & Aldrich, Huntington; built 1905–07; demolished in the 1950s. K: "Matinecock," J. P. Morgan, Jr., Residence, by La Farge & Morris, Glen Cove; built 1913; demolished 1980. L: "Beacon Towers," Mrs. O. H. P. Belmont House, by Hunt & Hunt, Sands Point; built ca. 1917; demolished 1943. M: General Nathaniel Woodhull House, Mastic; built ca. 1750; demolished ca. 1960s. N: Bathhouses, by William Muschenheim, Hampton Bays; built 1930; demolished 1954.

M

N

189

ARCHI AWARD BUILDINGS IN NASSAU AND SUFFOLK COUNTIES

WHY THE ARCHI AWARDS?

*I*n the middle sixties, Fred and Maria Bentel and I were chatting about the poor quality of architecture being produced on Long Island. Our concerns were not baseless.

In a humorous vein we envisaged an awards program for the worst architecture. Naturally, this would be an impossibility, since no budget could provide enough for the number of awards, and legal implications curtailed further discussion.

Nevertheless, the Long Island Association of Commerce and Industry became aware of the need to establish a real awards program and in 1964 sent out invitations for submissions. The requests, however, were addressed to owners rather than to architects, and the quality of the entries was, in most instances, rather mediocre. Yet the seed was planted and the program grew.

Then the Long Island Chapter of the AIA entered the picture, and the criteria for entries began to improve. Architects were being stimulated to enter. The awards were better publicized and the community was beginning to feel the impact of better architecture. Owners were more interested in having their projects win awards. Competition became more intense. Presentations, photographs and attitudes improved. The Archi Awards committee and the judges grew in stature, the awards ceremonies becoming a major event on Long Island.

The awards program has had a positive impact on Long Island's architecture. Those architects with a design conscience are expanding their careers with awards in mind. Several Long Island projects have attained awards at the state level. From here it is onward and upward.

WALTER E. BLUM
Former Member,
Board of Directors,
AIA, Long Island Chapter

ALBERTSON
Coventry town houses; Leonard Kurkowski (1988: Excellence).
Office building; Edwin J. Aviles (1970: First Prize).

AMAGANSETT
Haupt residence; Gwathmey, Siegel (1980).
Residence renovation; Frederick Stelle (1991).

A: Haupt residence, Amagansett.

AMITYVILLE
Amityville Public Library; Bentel & Bentel (1973: Silver).

ASHAROKEN
L. Pecchio residence; Norkatis & Olson (1974: Silver).

BABYLON
Harbor Club Garden Apartments; Siegmund Spiegel (1970).

BAY SHORE
Bay Shore Senior Citizens' Residence, Feldman & Kronia (1975).

BELLPORT
Bellport Animal Hospital; Robert A. W. Heins (1972: Silver).

BETHPAGE
Equitable Life Assurance Society; Wiedersum Associates (1971: Silver).

BLUE POINT
Harbour at Blue Point; Ira D. Haspel (1986: Gold).
Our Lady of the Snow Catholic Church; Wiedersum Associates (1969).

BRENTWOOD
Architect's office building; Dobiecki & Beattie (1969).

BRIDGEHAMPTON
° Sam's Creek Development houses; Norman Jaffe (1980).

BROOKVILLE
Facilities Service Building, Long Island University, C. W. Post Campus; R. J. Kaier & Associates (1975).

° *See also* entry in main text.

° Student Union Building, Long Island University, C. W. Post Campus; Bentel & Bentel (1974: Gold).

CARLE PLACE
Chase Manhattan Bank; Skidmore, Owings & Merrill (1970).
Country Glen Shopping Center; Spector Group (1988: Merit).

CEDARHURST
St. Joachim R.C. Church; F. J. Cashin / E. M. McCarron (1972: Silver, Interiors).

CENTERPORT
Ullian residence; Philip C. Pandolphi (1980).

CENTRE ISLAND
Pegno residence; Bentel & Bentel (1983).
Residence; Bentel & Bentel (1991).

B: Pegno residence, Centre Island.

191

COLD SPRING HARBOR
°Oliver and Lorraine Grace Auditorium; Centerbrook Architects (1987: Gold).

COMMACK
Bank of Smithtown; Coyler & Post (1973: Silver).

Guardian Federal Savings; Lo-Pinto, Pisani & Falco (1972: Silver).

COPIAGUE
South Shore Federal Savings & Loan; Wiedersum Associates (1975).

DIX HILLS
Dix Hills Park Ice-Skating Rink; Ward Associates (1975: Gold).

DOUGLASTON
Douglaston Associates; Walter Blum (1966).

EAST HAMPTON
°Gates of the Grove Synagogue (Jewish Center of the Hamptons); Norman Jaffe (1988: Design Citation).

Gruzen residence; Jordan Gruzen (1985: Honorable Mention).

Hardscrabble residence; Robert A. M. Stern (1987: Gold).

Hillman residence; Norman Jaffe (1984: Honorable Mention).

C: Hillman residence, East Hampton.

Schmidt residence; Ronald H. Schmidt (1982).

EAST HILLS
Dante's Beauty Salon; Mojo-Stumer Associates (1982: Interiors).

Eugene Goldman residence; Alvin Jay Cohen (1972: Silver).

EAST MEADOW
°Nassau County Medical Center; Max O. Urbahn (1974: Silver).

Seaman's Bank for Savings; Carson, Lundin & Thorson (1976: Silver).

EAST NORWICH
Tower Square Shops; George LeBrun (1986: Silver).

EAST PATCHOGUE
Apartment complex; Samuel Paul (1976: Silver).

EAST QUOGUE
Hirschorn residence; Hobart Betts (1979).

EAST ROCKAWAY
Bankers Trust Company; Edwards & Malone (1969).

FARMINGVILLE
Allstate Insurance Co.; Michael Harris Spector (1980).

FIRE ISLAND
Fire Island Telephone; Rose, Beaton & Rose (1976: Silver).

Pedateila beach house; Robert A. W. Heins (1976).

FISHERS ISLAND
Residence; Herbert Beckhard (1984: Honorable Mention).

Residence; James Volney Righter (1986: Honorable Mention).

FRANKLIN SQUARE
Paul Anthony Aesthetics; Mojo-Stumer (1986: Interiors).

FREEPORT
Freeport Street Mall; Bernard Rothzeid & Partners (1979).

GARDEN CITY
°Ruth S. Hartley University Center, Adelphi University; Warner Burns Toan & Lunde (1971: Silver).

Long Island Trust Co.; Wiedersum Associates (1970).

°Norstar Bank; Bentel & Bentel (1972: Silver).

666 Old Country Road office building; Michael Harris Spector (1982).

GLEN COVE
Dosoris Estates residential development; Alfred DeVido (1970).

Glen Cove Boy's Club; Bentel & Bentel (1979: Silver).

Glen Cove Village Square; Joseph Zito, Jr. (1979).

°St. Hyacinth R.C. Church; Bentel & Bentel (1988: Excellence).

GREAT NECK
Gilcrest residence; Blum & Nerzig (1975).

Great Neck Municipal Firehouse; Mojo-Stumer (1990).

Great Neck Park Community Facilities Building; Blum & Nerzig (1975).

Great Neck Park District Administration Building; Walter Blum (1967).

D: Great Neck Park District Administration Building.

°Great Neck Public Library; Gibbons, Heidtman and Salvador (1970).

Great Neck Public Library Youth Facility ("Levels"); Michael Harris Spector (1974: Silver, Interiors).

Great Neck Shopping Tower; Michael Harris Spector (1973: Silver).

Hadley Mews Housing; Ronald Goodman (1980).

Hamburg Savings Bank; Wiedersum Associates (1974).

Hastings Tile & Pavement Co.; Mojo-Stumer (1984: Silver, Interiors).

Office building; Michael Harris Spector (1974: Silver).

Solar office building; Blum & Nerzig (1979).

Squire Restaurant; Michael Harris Spector (1970).

Ten Cutter Mill Road offices; Blum & Nerzig (1972: Silver).

Third Dimension Haircutters; Mojo-Stumer (1984: Interiors).

Thomaston Park; Ronald Goodman (1980).

Town-house residences; Ronald Goodman (1983).

GREENVALE
Iselin Library Center, Greenvale School; Harold Buttrick (1972: Silver).

HAMPTON BAYS
Witkin residence; Dobiecki & Beattie (1973: Silver).

HAUPPAUGE
Bank of Suffolk County; Michael Harris Spector (1974: Silver).

Barron's Educational Series, Inc.; Mojo-Stumer (1987: Masonry Institute Award).

LNR Communications; Angelo Francis Corva (1984).

New York State Office Building; Handren & Sharp (1974: Silver).

HEMPSTEAD
Echo Park Pool; Keith Hibner (1973: Silver).

Hempstead Town Hall; Heidelberger Associates (1969).

Hofstra University Library; Warner Burns Toan & Lunde (1967: Top Prize).

E: Hofstra University Library, Hempstead.

Hofstra University Life Science Center; Slingerland & Bloss (1971: Gold).

F: Hofstra University Life Science Center, Hempstead.

Hofstra University Student Center; Warner Burns Toan & Lunde (1967).

Holiday Inn Hotel; Michael Harris Spector (1972: Silver).

HEWLETT BAY PARK
Katz residence; Wax Bryman Associates (1975).

HICKSVILLE
Manufacturers Hanover Trust; Spector group (1984).

HOLBROOK
Grumman Data Systems; Spector Group (1985: Silver).

G: Grumman Data Systems, Bethpage.

HUNTINGTON
Huntington Magnetic Resonance Imaging; Joseph Matthews (1986: Interiors).

Huntington office building; Mojo-Stumer (1983).

Island Engine & Parts Company; Hoffman Grayson (1986).

North Shore residence; Gary D. Cannella Associates (1986: Gold).

Superior Surgical Manufacturing Co.; Norkaitis & Olson (1976: Silver).

Village East Profession Center; Howard Phillips (1979).

JERICHO
D. E. Axinn residence and office; Alvin Jay Cohen (1969).

Jericho Atrium offices; Peter Elkin (1986: Gold; Recycling).

Jericho Public Library; Bentel & Bentel (1974: Silver).

JONES BEACH
Boardwalk Restaurant; Skidmore, Owings & Merrill (1967).

KING'S POINT
Residence; Mojo-Stumer (1989).

LAKE GROVE
Smith Haven Mall; Copeland, Novak & Israel (1969).

LAKE SUCCESS
Garfinkle residence; Blum & Nerzig (1975).

Lake Success Community Facilities Building; Blum & Nerzig (1973: Silver).

Michelin National Headquarters; Gordon Powers & Associates (1969: Gold).

Village of Lake Success Golf Facility Building; Walter Blum (1968).

H: Village of Lake Success Golf Facility Building.

LATTINGTOWN
John Gambling residence; Bentel & Bentel (1974: Silver).

Pool pavilion, Oberlin residence; Bentel & Bentel (1983).

LIDO BEACH
Long Beach High School; Donald Z. Bailey (1971: Silver).

Playground and pavilion, Lido Beach Town Park; Ward Associates (1979).

I: Pool pavilion, Oberlin residence, Lattingtown.

LINDENHURST
Industrial Production Emp. Fund Building (now Omni Surgical); Bernard A. Marson (1971: Silver).

New York Telephone; Paul L. Wood & Associates (1969).

LOCUST VALLEY
House addition; Paul W. Erdman (1991).

Pool house; Innocenti & Webel / Kenneth W. Dowd (1991).

LONG BEACH
Multi-Model Transportation Center; Duchscherer Oberst Design (1988: Merit).

MANHASSET
Manhasset–Lakeville Firehouse; Spector Group (1988: Masonry).

J: Manhasset–Lakeville Firehouse, Manhasset.

Nubest & Co.; Mojo-Stumer (1983).

Shelter Rock Public Library; Bentel & Bentel (1970: Silver).

MEDFORD
Birchwood at Blue Ridge condominium; Siegmund Spigcel (1974: Silver).

MELVILLE
°Estée Lauder Laboratories; Davis, Brody & Associates / Richard Dattner & Associates (1967).

Chemical Bank; Eggers Group, PC (1972: Silver).

Long Island Trust; Spector Group (1991).

°*See also* entry in main text.

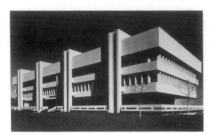

K: Chemical Bank, Melville.

MERRICK
South Shore Gastroenterology Medical Building; Mojo-Stumer (1985: Gold).

MIDDLE ISLAND
Village on Artist Lake; Jarmul & Brizee (1975).

MONTAUK
Krieger residence; Norman Jaffe (1979).

L: Krieger residence, Montauk.

Montauk Golf & Racquet Club; Richard Foster (1969: Top Prize).
°Montauk Manor condominium conversion; Bernard A. Marson (1971: Silver).
Villas at Montauk Golf & Racquet Club; Richard Foster (1973: Silver).

NEW HYDE PARK
Jewish Institute for Geriatric Care; Katz, Waisman & Weber (1976: Gold).

NORTH BELLPORT
Iverson Cycle Corporation; Gencorelli & Salo (1975).

NORTH HILLS
Spector Group offices; Michael Harris Spector (1976: Interiors).
Spector Group offices; Spector Group (1984).
3333 New Hyde Park Road; Michael Harris Spector (1975).

OAKDALE
Dowling College student housing; Slingerland Architects (1974: Silver).

OLD WESTBURY
Frankel residence; Mojo-Stumer (1986: Honorable Mention).

°*See also* entry in main text.

Locker facilities/offices, New York Institute of Technology; Bentel & Bentel (1971: Silver).
Nelson Rockefeller Academic Center, New York College of Osteopathic Medicine, New York Institute of Technology; Bentel & Bentel (1980).
Nussdorf residence; Mojo-Stumer (1985: Honorable Mention).

M: Nussdorf residence, Old Westbury.

Residence; Bentel & Bentel (1990).

OYSTER BAY
Neitlich residence; Bentel & Bentel (1971: Silver).

PATCHOGUE
St. Joseph's College Library; Bentel & Bentel (1990: Honorable Mention).

PLAINVIEW
Alina Corporation; Bentel & Bentel (1964: Grand Prize).
Bankers Trust Co.; Robert D. Nostrand (1969: Second Place).
Eastern Savings Bank; Michael Harris Spector (1975).

PLANDOME
North Shore Unitarian School; Bentel & Bentel (1967: Grand Prize).

N: North Shore Unitarian School, Plandome.

PORT JEFFERSON
North Shore Jewish Center; Landow & Landow (1975).
Strump residence; Edward Miller (1983).

PORT WASHINGTON
Don Primi & Associates, Inc., Offices; Mojo-Stumer Associates (1982).

N.P.D. Research Group; Peter Elkin (1984).
The Publishers Clearing House; Richard Foster (1984).
Unitarian senior housing; Walter E. Blum (1984: Honorable Mention).

QUOGUE
°Crowell residence and studio; Mark Simon, Centerbrook (1984; Gold).
Private residence; Hobart Betts (1984: Silver).
Wietz residence; Gwathmey, Siegel & Associates (1980).

RIVERHEAD
LILCO Operations Center; LILCO (1970).

ROCKVILLE CENTRE
First National City Bank; Charles Luckman Associates (1967; Third Prize).

RONKONKOMA
Equipark Industrial Mall; Artek Associates (1979).
Quality King II Industrial Building; Mojo-Stumer (1989).

ROOSEVELT FIELD
Union Dime Savings Bank; William Berger Associates (1979).

ROSLYN
Avant Garde Optics; Michael Harris Spector (1982).
Expressway Office Center; Michael Harris Spector (1971: Silver).
486 Willis Avenue; Mojo-Stumer (1983).
Ponemon residence; Guy Ladd Frost (1974).
°Roslyn Highlands Firehouse; Spector Group (1986: Gold).

SANDS POINT
Blankman residence; Bentel & Bentel (1975: Silver).

SAYVILLE
St. Lawrence Church; Dobiecki & Beattie (1971: Silver).
Sayville Nursing Home; Landow & Landow (1970).

SEA CLIFF
Residence; Wayne Ehmann (1989).
Sea Cliff beach pavilion; Wayne Ehmann Associates (1987: Gold).
Speranza/Ehmann offices; Wayne Ehmann (1988).

SELDEN
New York Telephone Radio Communications Building; Rose, Beaton & Rose (1971: Silver).
St. Joseph Village for Senior Citizens; Kaeyer, Parke & Garment (1980).

Selden Firehouse; T. J. Biuso & R. W. Barry (1972: Silver).

Smithtown Science Building, Suffolk Community College; Dobiecki & Beattie (1969: Second Place).

Southampton Building, Suffolk Community College; Dobiecki & Beattie (1973: Silver).

SHOREHAM

Fred Abeles residence: Beatty & Beatty (1975).

St. Mark's Church; Beatty & Beatty (1979).

SMITHTOWN

Accompsett Junior High School; James Lothrop (1972: Silver).

Baum, Skigen & Lefkowitz offices; Landau & Landau (1975).

Smithtown High School West; Lothrop Associates (1973: Gold).

O: Smithtown High School West.

SOUND BEACH

°St. Louis de Montfort Church; Lawrence L. Smith Associates (1980).

SOUTHAMPTON

Arnold residence; Norman Jaffe (1985: Bronze).

P: Arnold residence, Southampton.

° *See also* entry in main text.

East End Suffolk village house; David Chang of E.S.I. Associates (1971: Silver).

Froebel beach house; Robert A. Heins (1976: Silver).

Galeza residence; Andrew Tesoro (1987: Gold).

Reese residence; William J. Reese (1988: Design Citation).

Revco, Inc., headquarters; Peter Elkin (1986: Silver, Recycling).

Southampton guest house; James Volney Righter (1986: Gold).

STONY BROOK

Student housing, State University of New York at Stony Brook; Milton Petrides (1983).

SYOSSET

North Shore Atrium; Peter Elkin (1980).

UNIONDALE

°EAB Plaza; Spector Group (1985: Honorable Mention).

Nassau Veterans Memorial Coliseum; Welton Becket (1972: Gold).

Nassau West Corporate Center; Mojo-Stumer (1985: Honorable Mention).

VALLEY STREAM

Dime Savings Bank of New York; Wiedersum Associates (1974: Silver).

WAINSCOTT

Keller residence; Frederick Stelle (1987: Historic Preservation).

WANTAGH

Water-pollution control plant; Consoer & Morgan (1974: Silver).

WATER MILL

Gelb residence; Paul Segal Associates (1987: Gold).

Residence; Paul Segal Associates (1986: Silver).

Residence at Half Creek; Robert A. M. Stern (1988: Design Citation).

WESTBURY

Local 115 Union building; Gilbert & Associates (1984).

Fred the Furrier's Fur Vault; Mojo-Stumer (1987: Interiors).

WESTHAMPTON

Kislevitz residence; Gwathmey, Siegel (1979: Silver).

WEST ISLIP

West Islip Public Library; Gibbons & Heidtman (1969).

Q: West Islip Public Library.

WOODBURY

Crossways Office Building; Michael Harris Spector (1973: Silver).

WOODMERE

Woodmere Academy Learning Center; Bentel & Bentel (1975: Silver).

R: Woodmere Academy Learning Center.

National *AIA* Award Winners on *Long Island*

1963

Mr. & Mrs. Marshall Safir residence, Kings Point; George Nemeny.

A: Safir residence, Kings Point.

B: Matthews residence, East Hampton.

1968

Hale Matthews residence, East Hampton; Alfred DeVido.

1971

*Estée Lauder Laboratories, Melville; Davis, Brody & Associates/Richard Dattner & Associates (joint venture).

1978

De Menil / Carpenter residence, East Hampton; Howard Barnstone.

1981

*Jones Laboratory, Cold Spring Harbor; Moore Grover Harper, PC.

1982

Residence, East Hampton; Eiserman Robertson Architects.

See also entry in main text.

196

Index

This index lists persons, businesses, buildings, constructions, monuments and estates mentioned in the captions to the illustrations. Streets, neighborhoods and other sites are not included. Unless otherwise specified, references are to caption numbers.